MW00800802

THE SCOTTISH HOUSE

THE SCOTTISH HOUSE

photographs by
IANTHE RUTHVEN
text by Ianthe & Malise Ruthven

COLLINS & BROWN

NK
2045
A1
R88
2000

LIBRARY
NORTHERN VIRGINIA COMMUNITY COLLEGE

For Wendy

First published in Great Britain in 2000 by
Collins & Brown Limited, London House, Great Eastern Wharf,
Parkgate Road, London SW11 4NQ

Distributed in the United States and Canada by Sterling Publishing Co,
387 Park Avenue South, New York, NY 10016, USA

Copyright © Collins & Brown Limited 2000
Text copyright © Ianthe Ruthven 2000
Photographs copyright © Ianthe Ruthven 2000

The right of Ianthe Ruthven to be identified as the author of this
work has been asserted by her in accordance with the
Copyright, Designs and Patents Act, 1988.

A CIP catalogue record of this book is available from the British Library.

ISBN 1-85585-805-3

All rights reserved. No part of this publication may be reproduced,
stored in a retrieval system, or transmitted, in any form or by any means,
electronic, mechanical, photocopying, recording or otherwise, without
the written permission of the publishers and copyright holders.

1 3 5 7 9 8 6 4 2

PROJECT EDITOR: Ulla Weinberg
EDITOR: Alison Wormleighton
DESIGNER: Luise Roberts
INDEX: Ingrid Lock

Reproduced in London/Great Britain by Bluetag Ltd
Printed and bound in Hong Kong by Dai Nippon Printing Co (HK)

Houses open to the public

The following houses are open to the public during the months specified. It is advisable to check opening days and hours with the house beforehand.
Arthur Lodge: Wed./Sat. in June/July, and Wed. in Aug./Sept. Tel: 0131 667 5163; **Cawdor Castle:** Apr. 1–Sept. 30. Tel: 01667 404615; **Delgatie Castle:** Apr. 2–Oct. 24. Tel: 01888 563479; **Drumlanrig Castle:** May–Sept. Tel: 01848 330248; **The Hill House:** Apr. 1–Oct. 31. Tel: 01436 673900; **Hopetoun House:** Apr.–Sept. Tel: 0131 331 2451; **Mount Stuart:** Apr. 22–Sept. 30 (not Tues./Thurs.). Tel: 01700 503877; **Stobhall:** Gardens, grounds and chapel, last week in May and most of June; **Tenement House:** Mar. 1–Oct. 31. Tel: 0141 333 0183; **Traquair House:** Apr. 1–Oct. 31. Tel: 01896 830323.

Acknowledgments

I would like to thank the owners of all the houses I photographed, without whose cooperation, patience and unfailing hospitality this book would never have happened. The manner in which everyone entered into the spirit of the enterprise, helping in ways far beyond welcoming us into their homes to turn them upside down, was greatly appreciated. These included thoughtful suggestions, practical advice and, most of all, invaluable contributions to the text, without which I would still be struggling today.

In addition, a special thanks to the following who gave their time unstintingly, often accompanied by generous hospitality, for no better reason than a love of Scotland and Scottish houses: Geordie and Patricia Burnett-Stuart, Prof. David Walker, Mary Miers, David and Sarah Gilmour, Ian and Mary Dunlop, Peter and Chloe Ford, Nick and Limma Groves-Raines, John Batty, Alistair and Kate Robertson, Robert Dalrymple, Admiral Sir Roderick Macdonald, Mark Johnson, Ros and Jeremy Holmes, Alex and Annabel Urquhart, Andrew Thriepland, Roger Banks, Holly Eley, Domenica More Gordon, James Simpson, Sarah Anderson, Selina Fox, Patrick Bowe, Nicola Gordon Bowe, Colin Lindsay Macdougal, Maggie and Bill Williams, Hugh Poole Warren, Jean and Sandy Lindzay, Charles Gwyn, Irene Maclaran, Andy Macmillan, Hugo Fraser, Michael Horne, Dawn Balharry, Charles and Fiona Ward-Jackson, Catriona Stewart, Kirsty Burrell, Jimmy Thomson, Magnus and Veronica Linklater, Peter and Claudia Ferguson-Smyth, Peter and Shaunagh Ward-Jackson and Bill Brogden. Finally, a very special thanks to Adrian and Auriol Linlithgow, who kindly let me stay at Hopetoun House while researching and photographing for this book.

Thanks to Ulla Weinberg and Kate Kirby at Collins and Brown for their encouragement during the production process; to Luise Roberts, the designer, for her patience; and to Alison Wormleighton for her helpful suggestions with the text.

Captions

HALF TITLE PAGE: *A glimpse of the atrium from the garden room at Arthur Lodge, Edinburgh, showing the stair balusters and a bust of Mary Queen of Scots. The doors are hung with panels of old Venetian embroidery.*

FRONTISPIECE: *Part of the living room of a renovated sixteenth-century tower-house on the outskirts of Edinburgh.*

TITLE PAGE: *A display of French muzzle-loading flintlock muskets at Cawdor Castle. It commemorates the Fishguard invasion by a French expeditionary force on February 22, 1797. The French surrendered unconditionally when they came face to face with the 1st Lord Cawdor, backed by his yeomanry troops and the local volunteer force.*

PAGES 12–13: *View of Stalker Castle on the Argyll coast.*

PAGES 44–5: *View from the rooftop of Drumlanrig Castle, Dumfriesshire.*

PAGES 82–3: *Crovie village near Banff on the north coast of Aberdeenshire.*

PAGES 106–7: *The drawing room of Charles Rennie Mackintosh's Hill House in Helensburgh.*

PAGES 140–1: *Charles Jencks's landscaped garden at Portrack in Dumfriesshire.*

CONTENTS

ABOVE: *A convex Regency mirror in the drawing room at Arthur Lodge, Edinburgh*

INTRODUCTION

OPPOSITE: *Detail of the serving room at Drumlanrig showing an 1817 portrait of Joseph Florence, chef, by John Ainslie. Much appreciated by Sir Walter Scott, it shows him proudly displaying his menu containing such items as* Gratin à la Boudin à la Drumlanrig, Croquette à la Côtelette de Montagu, *and* Petit pains à la Duchesse. *Above is a portrait of Dr Graham Dalkeith.*

LEFT: *A view from the courtyard to the 'street' of outbuildings, which form part of the original steading (farmstead) at Melsetter House, Orkney.*

BELOW: *A renovated bedroom at an old manse (Presbyterian minister's house), near Edinburgh, which has been decorated with a subtle, minimalist New England flavour, while carefully preserving the old fabric of the house.*

A DISTINGUISHED SCOTTISH ARCHITECT, Sir Robert Rowand Anderson, whose splendid neo-Gothic palace at Mount Stuart on the Isle of Bute is celebrated in this book, described the essential character of Scottish architecture in his book *The Place of Architecture in the Domain of Art*, published in 1889:

> *If you examine the plans of an old Scottish mansion, you can read it like a storybook from the foundations to the chimney tops. You can distinguish the original tower that the family once lived in… You will then notice an addition when the family became richer and times were less warlike… It was never built solely to look picturesque or interesting… It was built from time to time to suit the necessities of the day.*

The exterior configuration of any house or castle not only reflects its owners' position in the world, but also makes a statement about their beliefs and aspirations. The forbidding towers and crow-stepped gables of the late medieval period were modified by the import of French detailing, particularly from the Loire châteaux. The combination of styles, with its distinctive ornamentation, established a recognizably Scottish vernacular. In 1707, however, the Union of Parliaments drew the Scottish elite ever more closely into the orbit of English culture and taste, and the classicism of Edinburgh's New Town and the Adam family gave the Union its formal architectural expression. Later, the nineteenth-century 'Baronial' revivals, expressing the new, romanticized version of Scottish history and identity popularized by Sir Walter Scott, revitalized the older traditions. They created a kind of dialogue in stone between Gothic heart and neoclassical head; between the visionary wings of the Scottish psyche and the pragmatic rationalism of its intellect.

The currents of history and fashion influence the interior arrangements of buildings, in similar, but much

OPPOSITE: *The hall at Melsetter House, Orkney, showing W R Lethaby's fireplace and sandstone chimney breast.*

RIGHT: *The eighteenth-century mantelpiece in the Traquair House drawing room.*

BELOW: *The chimney piece and overmantel in the drawing room at Mount Stuart on the Isle of Bute.*

more complex, interesting and idiosyncratic ways. Like Anderson's mansion, interior furnishings may reflect a family's evolution from a condition of frugality to affluence. But they may just as well tell the opposite story – the downward mobility occasioned by loss of land and the constant struggles to keep out the damp and repair the roof.

The British artist Richard Hamilton claimed that any interior is '… a set of anachronisms, a museum, with the lingering residues of decorative styles that an inhabited space collects …'. In the houses represented here, the patina of accumulation, the arrangement of objects garnered over generations or a single lifetime, offer glimpses into personal histories – or into history rendered personal by physical association, like the bed allegedly slept in by Mary Queen of Scots at Traquair. Cherished family heirlooms, some priceless, others valueless to any but their owners, are vital links to the past, whether this be the magnificent cabinets at Drumlanrig given to the Duke of Monmouth by his natural father, Charles II, or a curious piece of driftwood gathered from a beach in Tiree.

The castles, houses and cottages in this book are not necessarily representative, either historically or aesthetically. They have been chosen above all for their owners' distinctive approach – and to give the lie to the perception, widely held among the English, that the Scots are lacking in taste and creature comforts. As the architectural historian Ian Gow pointed out in 1992:

The tenacious conventional view remains that the Scots forswore everything that smacked of luxury in their houses under the influence of John Knox and that their only contribution to interior design had to await the genius of Charles Rennie Mackintosh… In fact, nothing can be further from the truth and, if trouble is taken to look, there is plenty of evidence to show that the Scots were no less interested in the comfort and beauty of their houses than any other nation in Europe.

The houses shown in this book all testify to the accuracy of this statement. The first chapter, *Towers of Fortitude*, shows five historic houses that originated as tower-houses, the fortified domestic structures that appeared at the end of the thirteenth century and gradually died out in the sixteenth. They embodied a feudal social system which, under weak central authority, allowed rival chiefs and their clansmen to vent their hostilities against each other. Three of those featured here – Cawdor Castle, Traquair and Stobhall – enjoy the intimacy of continuous family occupation.

In the second chapter, *Visions of Splendour*, practicality gives ground to display, as those landowning families who survived the turbulent politics of the sixteenth and seventeenth centuries

became fervent supporters of the Union and the British Crown, and benefited accordingly. Drumlanrig Castle, seat of the Dukes of Buccleuch and Queensberry, marks the transition from fortified dwelling to stately home, while nevertheless preserving in its interior the feeling of a family residence. Hopetoun, 'Scotland's Versailles', is, like Drumlanrig, a kind of hybrid – in this case between the seventeenth-century intimacy of Sir William Bruce's original building and the grandeur of the state rooms designed by William Adam and his sons, intended for ostentatious display rather than comfort. An even grander 'vision of splendour', one that exhausts superlatives with its deliberate transcendental overtones, is represented by Mount Stuart. This Puginesque Italian Gothic fantasy was

OPPOSITE: *With its soft white panelling, low-relief mouldings and plaster frieze of indigenous flowers, the drawing room at Melsetter House, Orkney, has a light and airy feel.*

BELOW: *Detail of the sitting room of a restored fisherman's cottage in Cromarty in the north-east Highlands. The tongue-and-groove panelling covers the stairs.*

designed in the nineteenth century by Sir Robert Rowand Anderson for the 3rd Marquess of Bute, reputedly the richest man in Britain. Incorporating state-of-the-art Victorian technology, Mount Stuart appeared as a fully formed domestic environment with the outward appearance of the Victorian Railway Terminus in Bombay: a 'thematic house' that anticipates the 'New Age' zeitgeist promoted by such contemporary architects as Michael Graves and Charles Jencks. A late eighteenth-century precedent exists in Cairness House, James Playfair's neglected neoclassical masterpiece inspired by French revolutionary ideas, and set, improbably, in the bleak Buchan countryside, as remote from the urban bustle of Aberdeen as it is from the majestic Grampian mountains.

The third chapter, *Casting Adrift*, turns away from castles and palaces to explore some traditional dwellings around Scotland's thousands of miles of coastline. On the Isle of Tiree, outermost of the Inner Hebrides, the artist Kirsty Laird has restored two 'black-houses', which she has filled with *objets trouvés* from the beaches of this windiest of islets. On the Orkney Mainland, painters Peter McLaren and Arlene Isbister have converted their old long-house with exceptional flair and sensitivity. On the Isle of Skye, the Fishing Lodge at Camasunary preserves the memory of a sport now threatened by chemicals and fish farming. In the former fishing village of Crovie, near Banff, abandoned by its inhabitants after a devastating storm in 1953, a group of incomers has bought up and restored numerous cottages in what is now recognized as one of the finest examples of an eighteenth-century fishing village in Europe. And finally in the western Highlands, The Square, Roshven, recently restored to its original state, shows how tongue-and-groove panelling and subtly mixed colours can be used to

enhance the sense of space in a small cottage made entirely out of concrete.

The fourth chapter, *Urbane Originals*, pays tribute to the imagination and quality of design to be found (by those persistent enough to look) in Scotland's towns and two great cities. While Charles Rennie Mackintosh's Hill House in Helensburgh was the last word in innovative sophistication a century ago, Arthur Lodge, in Edinburgh, is a brilliant evocation of the neoclassicism adopted by a city that, in the early nineteenth century, aspired to be the 'Athens of the North'. Also in Edinburgh, Emma Hawkins at Atholl Crescent emulates Queen Victoria at Balmoral by supporting the taxidermy trade. Even the most exotic stuffed birds and animals benefit from the space and

light afforded by her finely proportioned Regency terraced house. While the Highlands are rarely associated with the refinements of urban living, at Clifton House in Nairn, the Highland spirit, eclipsed by Culloden nearby, has been revived. Here, an exuberantly decorated private family hotel is devoted to excellence in food, wine, entertainment and company.

Inventive Traditions, the final chapter in this book, celebrates the referential qualities of Scottish domestic architecture, drawing on a wide range of borrowings and motifs, while setting its distinctive stamp upon them. At Kinlochmoidart in Invernesshire, William Leiper adapted the tower-house tradition to accommodate the leisurely pursuits of a rich Victorian family. At Killean on Kintyre, Sir John Burnet and his more famous pupil and son, John James Burnet, collaborated to produce a more eclectic version of Scottish Baronial, influenced by the Arts and Crafts movement and French ideas from the École des Beaux Arts. On the Island of Hoy in Orkney, W R Lethaby, one of the greatest exponents of the Arts and Crafts movement, adapted and enlarged the original laird's steading (farmstead) to create what must be one of the best-designed country houses in Britain. By way of contrast, two more 'traditional' houses – Ardpatrick and The Old Manor – demonstrate how, with a flair for fabrics, a good colour sense and a collector's eye, the omnipresent laird's house that is too often subjected to the conventional regimes of tassels, tartans and chintz can be completely transformed.

FORTITUDE

TOWERS OF FORTITUDE

CAWDOR CASTLE

ABOVE: *Cawdor Castle from the flower garden. The original tower-house, dating from the late 1300s, was built for defence. It consisted of four storeys and a keep house, with an entrance on the first floor.*

OPPOSITE: *The seventeenth-century tapestry behind the sideboard in the dining room shows a scene from Don Quixote by Cervantes. The tapestry was long thought to be Spanish, but recent research suggests it was made in London.*

CAWDOR CASTLE ON THE MORAY FIRTH, near Nairn, has a charm that belies the murderous, and ill-founded, reputation it received from its association with *Macbeth*. A rectangular keep was built in the 1450s, enclosing a tower-house dating from the late 1300s. That was no less than three and a half centuries after the events recorded in Holinshed's translation of Boethius's *History of Scotland*, which Shakespeare adapted to flatter King James VI and I in 1606. Nevertheless, Victorian visitors were treated to the *frisson* arising from being shown the four-poster bed in 'King Duncan's room', where Macbeth was supposed to have committed murder most foul on the sleeping monarch. The most celebrated of Shakespearean actors, Sir Henry Irving, made a special visit to Cawdor in 1887 with his leading lady, Ellen Terry, to 'absorb the atmosphere' for their production of the play.

The castle's fame as the seat of the Thanes of Cawdor for more than six centuries continues to attract 100,000 visitors a year. Despite the obvious temptations, the present

LEFT: *The old kitchen. Set in the basement close to the castle's well, the kitchen was in use between 1640 and 1938. The Victorian cooking range at the end has a mechanical spit turned by a fan in the flue. The cabinet on the right displays a variety of household devices such as clothing irons, warming pans and butter churns.*

ABOVE: *The front stairs with 'Campbell of Cawdor' tartan carpeting. A display of French guns captured in 1797 recalls the last invasion of mainland Britain, when a party of 1,400 French revolutionary troops landed at Fishguard in Pembrokeshire. Mistaking the red flannel dresses worn by Welsh women for English Redcoats, the French troops surrendered unconditionally to the local commander, the 1st Baron Cawdor.*

incumbent, Angelika Lady Cawdor, widow of the 25th Thane and 6th Earl, scrupulously eschews the Shakespearean hype indulged in by some of her predecessors. 'King Duncan's room' no longer features. The castle, however, still offers plenty of 'atmosphere'. The door to the tower leading from the courtyard is protected by a *bretasche*, or 'murder-hole', jutting from the main wall above it, through which fiery projectiles and boiling liquids could be showered over uninvited guests. The fifteenth-century drawbridge is still intact. With a little imagination it is possible to see the great courtyard beneath the tower as it must once have been – a refuge enclosed by thick, lofty walls where in times of trouble the whole clan could shelter, along with their barefoot children, poultry and cattle.

Donald, the 1st Thane of Cawdor for whom we have documentary evidence, appears as a witness to a legal document in 1295 – two and a half centuries after the reign of the historical Macbeth (1040–57). Donald's son William was confirmed in the title of Thane – which is a Saxon borrowing from the Norse title *thegn*, meaning 'trusted servant of the King' – by Robert the Bruce, or Robert I, the Scottish King, in 1310.

ABOVE: *The tower room on the first floor of Thane William's tower has the original entrance as one of its windows. The Flemish tapestries on the right of the photograph, which were woven in about 1630, depict the 'Arts & Sciences' of Rhetoric, Geography and Astronomy. Over the mantelpiece hangs a seascape by the eighteenth-century French landscape painter Joseph Vernet.*

RIGHT: *The drawing room, set in the great hall of the castle, dates from the sixteenth century or earlier. It took its present form in 1684, when the fireplace was installed, embellished with the Cawdor family emblems of a stag's head and buckle. The Chinese stoneware jar in the foreground dates from the Sung dynasty (960–1279 CE).*

The 3rd Thane, also William, is thought to have begun building the original tower-house around 1380. Legend has it that, following a dream, he tied a coffer of gold to the back of a donkey and allowed the animal to choose the spot where he would build his tower. The donkey eventually came to rest by the third of three hawthorns near the burn (small stream) that now runs by the castle. The Thane built around the tree, the stump of which has been preserved in the 'thorn tree room' in the basement. Radiocarbon dating gives an approximate date of 1372, consistent with the style of masonry at the bottom of the tower.

Major improvements and extensions were carried out by the 15th Thane, Sir Hugh Campbell, in the late seventeenth century. A cultivated and scholarly man, he employed no architects, preferring to supervise the masons himself. The tradition of sensitive improvements continued in the nineteenth century, by which time the thanes had acquired large estates in Wales, where they spent most of their time. The 19th Thane was created a baron; the 20th became the 1st Earl Cawdor. Cawdor escaped the 'Baronialization' that afflicted many other old Scottish castles during the Victorian era. Today, despite being open to the public for half the year, it succeeds in preserving the comfort and intimacy of a family house.

ABOVE: *The dining room. The chimney piece commemorates the marriage in 1510 between Sir John Campbell, younger son of the Earl of Argyll, and Muriel, daughter of the 8th Thane, who brought the castle into the Campbell family. Although she was kidnapped as an infant by her future father-in-law, the 'crossbow marriage' was surprisingly happy – and fruitful.*

DELGATIE CASTLE

OPPOSITE: *Delgatie, the Hay clan's family home for seven centuries, was purchased in 1957 by Captain Hay from his kinswoman. The dining room, which was restored at that time, contains furniture he brought from his original home in the Shetlands. The painting over the sideboard, by an unknown artist, depicts Moses welcoming his father from Egypt.*

LEFT: *Delgatie Castle stands on the foundations of an earlier fortress-keep dating from 1050. The present tower dates from the 1540s with the battlement walk above the string-course completed in 1579. Two wings – including a chapel and servants' quarters – were added in the 1740s.*

'THERE ARE IN SCOTLAND for the most part two strongholds to every league, intended both as a defence against a foreign foe, and to meet the first outbreak of a civil war,' wrote the fifteenth-century Scottish historian John Major. The gently undulating lowlands of Aberdeenshire, now mainly arable farms but once a barren hinterland remote from the centres of power, exemplify Major's observation. The county is studded with fortress-keeps, or tower-houses, in which feudal – and feuding – families protected themselves from the unwanted attentions of their neighbours.

Delgatie Castle, near Turriff, is a case in point. Its story, over almost ten centuries, reflects shards of Scotland's turbulent history like fragments of a mirror. The original eleventh-century tower was built by the Comyns, Earls of Buchan, and is incorporated in the present sixteenth-century structure. As supporters of the English King, they lost the castle after the Battle of Bannockburn in June 1314, when Robert the Bruce inflicted a bloody defeat on the knights of Edward II. The victorious Scottish King presented the castle to his right-hand man, Gilbert Hay, Hereditary Lord High Constable of Scotland, who gave it to his younger brother.

During the wars of the Reformation in the sixteenth century, the Hays, as Catholics, came into conflict with the King. After the Battle of Glenlivet in 1594, when the Hays and their allies the Gordons defeated the Protestant Campbells, James VI decided to teach his

DELGATIE CASTLE

OPPOSITE: *The newel,
or turnpike, staircase set
in the walls is the widest
of any Scottish castle.
Repairing its 97 steps was
the first task Captain Hay,
a trained mason, set
himself.*

BELOW: *The library just as
Captain Hay left it before
his death in 1997. At the
very top of the keep, it was
his favourite retreat.*

Catholic lords a lesson. He blew up the castles of Huntly and Slains, but at Delgatie he met the unexpected resistance of Andrew Hay's mistress Rohaise, a feisty 19-year-old with flaming red hair who organized the defence of the castle. The King was forced to bring two siege guns from Edinburgh; these were taken by sea to Banff and dragged overland by 30 yoke of oxen apiece. By the time the battered west wall of the castle had finally collapsed, Rohaise and her fellow-defenders had escaped to France and the King had too little powder left to demolish the castle. Three years later the Hays were pardoned and permitted to repair their castle, on one condition. The width of the new wall, previously three metres (10 feet) thick or more, was to be restricted to the length of an arrow, to ensure its inadequacy against an artillery attack.

The first shots of the Civil War in Scotland were fired nearby in 1639, when the Covenanters, under the command of Sir William Hay, routed the royalists at the 'Trot of Turriff', as the skirmish was known. Changing sides in 1644, Hay subsequently served as chief of staff to the royalist commander, the Marquess of Montrose. Both fell victim to the machinations of the Earl of Argyll (chief of the Campbells) and were convicted of treason against King Charles II, whom they had loyally served. While Montrose was hanged, drawn and quartered, Hay suffered the slightly less ignominious fate of being beheaded.

In 1743, two wings – comprising a new kitchen and servants' quarters to the east, and a chapel and 'doocot' (dovecote) to the west – were added to the castle, but loyalty to the Jacobites brought financial ruin to the family. In the nineteenth century Delgatie was already in a state of neglect and by the end of the Second World War, during which it had been occupied by troops rescued from Dunkirk, it was considered beyond repair. Years of neglect had ravaged the structure; water ran through the building and part of the roof had collapsed.

Fortunately in 1957 the owner, the Countess of Erroll, was persuaded to sell Delgatie to her kinsman, Captain John Hay. A veteran of the Indian Army, Captain Hay devoted the next 40 years to rescuing and restoring the ancient family home and seat of the clan of which he was chief. Trained as a mason with the Bombay Sappers, he did much of the work himself, helped by his wife Eve (who died in 1975) and Joan Johnstone, who now looks after the castle.

Today, the private charitable trust the Captain set up to preserve Delgatie for posterity is careful to maintain the family atmosphere. The smell of home-made scones permeates the draughty corridors; weddings are still held in the chapel, and the dining room can be hired for special lunches and dinners. Delgatie is no arid museum. Though the Captain has passed on, his presence is felt in every room.

OPPOSITE: *The blue bedroom. The mahogany four-poster bed, cradle and spinning wheel date from the early nineteenth century. A child is said to have appeared beside the cot of any visiting babies who cried during the night. Some of the soldiers who occupied the castle during the Second World War were so scared of ghosts that they preferred to sleep in the grounds.*

BELOW: *The painted ceiling beams at Delgatie, a characteristic feature of tower-houses, are considered among the finest in Scotland. They were painted between 1592 and 1597. After being hidden for generations under layers of paint, they were uncovered by Captain Hay in the 1950s.*

LIBERTON HOUSE

OPPOSITE: *The original oak beams in Liberton's great hall were exposed after fire and water damage allowed the new owners, Nick and Limma Groves-Raines to rip out an inappropriately ornate Victorian ceiling. A late seventeenth-century painted wooden panel of A Couple Looking at Music hangs above an early eighteenth-century Italian travelling cabinet with an inlaid ivory figurine. The walls are over a metre (three feet) thick.*

LEFT: *Liberton House from the back showing the steep tiled roof and uneven fenestration characteristic of Scottish lairds' houses. When Historic Scotland provided a restoration grant, they insisted on preserving many later additions, including the flat-roofed bay window leading into the kitchen. Nick and Limma transformed it by adding the pitched roof. A mixture of copperas pigment and limewash gives the harled walls their 'weathered' ochre colour.*

I N 1991, NICK AND LIMMA GROVES-RAINES were showing some friends a fine view of Edinburgh from the Pentland Hills when they spotted charred rafters showing through the roof of an old mansion. They discovered that the wreckage belonged to Liberton House, a sixteenth-century fortified house. The couple, who specialize in restoring old castles, were unable to resist the opportunity. However, their enquiries revealed a tangle of litigation almost as chaotic as the mess in the castle, where firefighters had ripped off the roof in order to direct their hoses at the source of a fire.

Having remained in the family of its original owners, the Gilmours, for nearly four centuries, Liberton had passed through the hands of various developers. Negotiations were afoot between the district council and the developers, who wanted to divide up the site into a country club and nursing home. One of the speculators had already gone bankrupt; another was doing time in jail. The planners were refusing to let the nursing home open until the main house had been restored. The fire was potentially catastrophic, as the castle had not been insured.

Thanks to the couple's intervention and generous grants from Historic Scotland, a scenario ending with certain demolition was averted. As soon as they had repaired the roof Nick and Limma tackled the old bakery and brewhouse so that they could relocate their architectural offices there. Next they created an apartment in the attic, in order to live on site and supervise the work. From the point of view of authenticity, the fire and

TOWERS OF FORTITUDE

LIBERTON HOUSE

RIGHT: *An old Persian plate hangs over a seventeenth-century Jacobean cabinet in the great hall. The gateleg table dates from the seventeenth century and the Scottish chairs from the late nineteenth century. In the kitchen beyond, above the chair, is a nineteenth-century Scottish papier-mâché lacquered clock inlaid with mother-of-pearl.*

BELOW: *Detail of the
original kitchen showing
the 1890s makeover, which
includes the window,
fireplace and tiles. A
portrait by Limma is
propped up on a late
nineteenth-century
Baronial chair. The
original sink can just be
seen under the window.*

RIGHT: *A bold red and
white American quilt adds
colour to the small sitting
room upstairs. A
seventeenth-century
Florentine cabinet stands
to the left of the fireplace
from the same period. The
carved marble fragment on
the mantelpiece was
rescued in the 1930s from
a ruined house in County
Down, Northern Ireland.*

subsequent deterioration of the interior fabric turned out to be a blessing. In their standard work on historic Scottish houses, MacGibbon and Ross (1892) detailed the architectural vandalism perpetrated on Liberton during the 1840s when 'to accommodate the fabric to the tastes of the period, nearly all of its ancient features were obliterated or concealed'. The old high-pitched roof had been removed, the gables heightened and a new storey added. The base of the turret and its adjoining entrance had been hidden by a 'large and incongruous porch', the rugged walls and massive arches covered up by lath and plasterwork, the fine old oak beams concealed behind ornate Victorian ceilings. A later refurbishment during the 1890s gave the castle an Arts and Crafts flavour.

The fire and water damage allowed Nick and Limma to rip out most of the trite and commonplace features, while preserving what was best in the Arts and Crafts restoration. To get the right cornices Nick took a mould from one of the few surviving seventeenth-century houses in Edinburgh's Old Town. To match the traces left on the upstairs walls, he had floorboards cut to irregular widths. Old Scottish timbers were replaced with the nearest equivalent – imported Siberian larch. No trouble or expense was spared, and after a narrow escape Liberton thrives again.

RIGHT: *This Victorian bath – one of a job lot bought in Dundee – spent several years languishing in the garden before being restored to its original use. The curved zinc canopy was repaired, and taps and shower-head added piecemeal. The sails of the model yacht, found in a Highland village, act as an unusual light diffuser.*

TOWERS OF FORTITUDE

LIBERTON HOUSE

BELOW: *View of the kitchen showing the shallow recessed arch and central window set into the end wall. The table was found in a house in East Lothian and was originally an ironing table. On the left is a Nobel cooking range. The painted grey-blue floorboards and the white walls offset the warm tones of the wood.*

TRAQUAIR HOUSE

ABOVE: *Traquair has changed little since the end of the seventeenth century, when the 4th Earl added the wings at either side and the wrought-iron gates and railings. The twelfth-century tower is incorporated into the left side of the house.*

OPPOSITE: *The main stone spiral staircase with the carved oak door portraying the Scottish unicorn and the English lion locked in combat. It was brought from the Maxwell family home, Terregles House, Dumfriesshire, which had close ties with Traquair for over 300 years. Terregles was demolished recently and many of its treasures are now at Traquair.*

'DOOL AN' SORROW HAE FA'EN TRAQUAIR, / An' the Yetts that were shut at Charlie's comin' / He vowed wad be opened nevermair / Till a Stuart King was crowned in Lunnon.' An anonymous ballad commemorates one of the more romantic episodes in Scottish history, Bonnie Prince Charlie's visit to his kinsman Charles Stuart, the 5th Earl of Traquair, in 1745 to enlist local Jacobites in the march south to invade England.

Traquair House, already ancient at the time of the ill-fated '45 rising, was once a royal residence for the early Scottish kings. Set in the Tweed Valley in Peeblesshire, the original, early twelfth-century tower served as a hunting lodge. In 1469, James III presented it to one of his favourites, his 'Master of Musick', William Rogers. But only nine years later, the hapless beneficiary was forced to sell the house to the King's uncle, the Earl of Buchan, who wanted it for his son, James Stuart. The derisory sum of 70 Scots Merks (£3 15s. 10d.) is recorded in a deed of sale preserved at Traquair. Soon afterwards, the malevolent Earl (nicknamed 'Hearty James') helped some other nobles string up Rogers, with several others, from Lauder Bridge, not far away. In this disconcerting way, James Stuart became the 1st Laird of Traquair, where his descendants still reside.

ABOVE: *A trompe-l'oeil still-life panel in the manner of Egbert van Heemskerk hangs over the fireplace in the still room. The porcelain includes famille rose (a type of Chinese porcelain), c. 1780, on the three lower shelves. The painted wooden panelling was installed in the eighteenth century by the 5th Earl.*

RIGHT: *The eighteenth-century library on the upper floor. In the cove are grisaille portrait busts of classical writers and philosophers used as a means of cataloguing the 3,000 or so books, among which are many rare and ancient volumes. The murals were restored in 1823 by the Edinburgh artist James West. The two globes, celestial and terrestrial, date from the eighteenth century.*

RIGHT: *An eighteenth-century leather-bound library chair with book-rest. Each book in the library carries the Traquair bookplate and has on its spine an exact indication of its corresponding shelf and place number. Many of the Catholic books were looted by a Presbyterian mob in 1688 and burnt in the marketplace at Peebles.*

BELOW: *In the twelfth-century tower is the king's room, where Mary Queen of Scots stayed on her visit to Traquair in 1566. The state bed, remodelled in the eighteenth century, was brought from Terregles House. The hand-stitched silk bed cover is said to have been worked by the Queen and four ladies-in-waiting. On the bedhead hangs the Queen's crucifix and her rosary.*

In 1566, Mary Queen of Scots and her husband, Lord Darnley, visited Traquair for a hunting expedition. It is recorded by the Queen's secretary that on this occasion their host, Sir John Stuart, who had been knighted at her marriage to Darnley and was Captain of the Queen's Guard, firmly rebuked Darnley for daring to refer to the Queen as a 'mare'. Ever the loyal servant, Sir John engineered the Queen's night escape from the Palace of Holyrood in Edinburgh the following year after the conspiracy against her by Protestant lords.

The 7th Laird, John Stuart, whose meteoric rise was matched only by his subsequent fall, was the first to carry out major building works. He acquired huge power – second only to the King – when he was made Lord High Treasurer of Scotland by Charles I, having been created Earl of Traquair in 1633, when only 33. But as Lord High Commissioner to the General Assembly of the Church, his downfall was sealed amid the bitter religious conflicts following the Reformation. His attempt to introduce the Episcopal (Anglican) liturgy into Scotland met with violent opposition. Trying to steer a middle course between King and Kirk, the Earl was distrusted by both sides. He was dismissed from his post, heavily fined and from 1641 confined to his estates.

It was at this time that he set about domesticating the castle. Eschewing the convenience of catching fish out of the window, he diverted the River Tweed to its present course. An extra storey, with ornamented dormer windows, was added, so that the projections of the old castle plan were covered under one steep roof, incorporating the twelfth-century tower. After the Civil War, in which he played a somewhat ambiguous role, the Earl aligned himself with the ill-fated Charles I and was taken

prisoner by the Cromwellians at the Battle of Preston in 1648. Four years' imprisonment in Warwick Castle ruined him. After his release he was reduced to begging in the streets of Edinburgh. His son, the 2nd Earl, made life still more difficult for the family by embracing the Old Faith; his second wife, Lady Anne Seton, helped establish a tradition of Catholicism which thrives at Traquair to this day. A concealed staircase was made leading from the room where Mass was celebrated in secret, to facilitate the priest's escape when the house was searched, as it frequently was.

Paradoxically, Traquair benefited from its owners' wholehearted espousal of the Stuarts' cause and of the Catholic faith. The family's support for the losing side in Scotland's turbulent politics meant that there was never enough money to lavish on grandiose enlargements to the house. Indeed, it has scarcely changed since acquiring its present form at the end of the seventeenth century.

Today Traquair's custodians are Catherine Maxwell Stuart, the 21st Laird. She and her mother, Flora Maxwell Stuart, widow of the 20th Laird, have succeeded in preserving the distinctive family atmosphere while opening the house to the visitors whose numbers assure the survival of what has justly been called 'The Oldest Continuously Inhabited House in Scotland'.

ABOVE: *A view of the drawing room with the perfectly preserved harpsichord dated 1651. The portrait is of the seventeenth-century English poet John Dryden, a Jacobite sympathizer. The overdoor portrays 'Drama' and is one of three gold-painted panels representing the Liberal Arts. They were commissioned by the 5th Earl in the mid-eighteenth century as part of an extensive programme of refurbishment.*

LEFT: *The overdoor on the left in the drawing room represents 'Art and Architecture'. It also incorporates the Traquair and Conyers coats-of-arms symbolizing the 5th Earl's marriage to Theresa Conyers. Devoted to her husband, Theresa insisted on sharing his cell in the Tower of London where he was confined for his part in the 1745 rising.*

STOBHALL

OPPOSITE: *A wide passageway was created at one end of the original chapel when it was adapted for secular use in 1578. Access to the castle is overseen by a seventeenth-century dummy-board of a lady with a broom, and a Japanese fish sign above the door. The decorated oak beams are part of the sixteenth-century conversion.*

LEFT: *A detail of the mid-seventeenth-century dower house from the courtyard, with an ancient yew tapered to the shape of a cypress in the foreground. It was built by the 2nd Earl, whose initials and arms, along with those of his wife, are carved over the door: EJP and CJP for Earl John Perth and Countess Jane Perth.*

HOME OF THE ILLUSTRIOUS DRUMMOND FAMILY (later the Earls of Perth) from the fourteenth century, Stobhall, near Perth, is full of mystery and surprises. With two queens and a royal mistress in the family, one might expect to find an imposing castle. Instead there are three small buildings – a fourteenth-century chapel, a late sixteenth-century castle and a seventeenth-century dower house – grouped around a grass courtyard, with a fourth, rebuilt as a library in the 1950s, tucked away beyond the chapel. The beautiful topiary gardens conjure up images of medieval courtly love: romance played a pivotal role in the family's fortunes.

In 1363, Malcolm Drummond's daughter, Margaret, married King David II, son of Robert the Bruce. Three years later her niece Arabella married the King's cousin, the Earl of Carrick, who in 1390 succeeded to the throne as Robert III, the first Stuart king of Scotland. Both women were famed for their beauty.

A few generations later another Drummond girl, Margaret, won the heart of a king – in this case James IV. 'Tayis Bank', a late fifteenth-century Scottish poem probably penned by the King himself, describes their meeting on the banks of the Tay below Stobhall: 'This myld, meik, mansuet Mergrit / This perle polist most quhyt / Dame Natouris deir dochter discreit / This dyamant of delyt.' The poem ends: 'Joy was within and joy without / Under that wlonkest waw / Quhair Tay ran down with stremis stout / Full strecht under Stobshaw.'

ABOVE: *The entrance hall to the chapel building.*

BELOW: *Detail of the early seventeenth-century ceiling decoration in the chapel. The figures represent the contemporary emperors and kings of Europe and North Africa.*

OPPOSITE: *The fourteenth-century chapel reverted to religious use when the 4th Earl converted to Catholicism in 1685. The altar window was put in by Clementina Drummond in the nineteenth century.*

ABOVE: *A few years after Lord and Lady Perth took over Stobhall in 1953, they built the library cum billiard room on the site of two tumbledown cottages, which had probably replaced the original fourteenth-century house. The bookcase pilasters are copied from those in the drawing room at Traquair House (see page 37) and are thus a visual allusion to the blood ties between the Drummond and Maxwell families.*

Margaret's father was showered with grants and offices and in 1488 was raised to the peerage. Margaret and the King, who probably married in secret, were certainly lovers for six years, until in 1502 Margaret and her two sisters died in suspicious circumstances. It is said they all ate a poisoned fish intended for Margaret by a party of nobles, who were planning for the King to marry Margaret Tudor, daughter of Henry VII.

In the latter part of the sixteenth century, the second Lord Perth and his wife, Dame Lilias Ruthven, remodelled the fourteenth-century chapel on the west side of Stobhall and built a small, three-storey castle on the north side. Succeeding generations of the family remained loyal to the Stuarts, and the title of Duke of Perth was conferred on the 4th Earl by the exiled James VII and II. With the failure of the 1715 and 1745 Jacobite risings, however, their estates were confiscated and were not restored until 1784.

In the nineteenth century, Stobhall became a retreat for sportsmen and artists, including Sir John Everett Millais. By then it had passed through the female line into the possession of the Ancaster family. In 1953 the last Earl of Ancaster gave Stobhall, which was in need of much repair, to the present Lord Perth. Stobhall and the Perth title were reunited after an interval of 150 years.

BELOW: *The eighteenth-century clock was rescued from Machany House (later Strathallan Castle) after the Battle of Culloden, when it was plundered by Hanovarian soldiers. 'One of the few relics is the kitchen clock, hacked by their swords and marked by bullet wounds,' wrote Lord Perth's grandmother, Viscountess Strathallan.*

ABOVE: *Commanding spectacular views over the River Tay, the octagonal folly was created by the present Lord Perth over the public convenience below. The seventeenth-century painted wooden panelling, by David McBeath of Edinburgh, came from a summerhouse that used to adjoin the brick-walled garden at Polton House (now demolished), south of Edinburgh. As it was originally designed for a square room, Stuart Todd, Lord Perth's architect, had a difficult time coaxing the panelling into its new, octagonal home.*

SPLENDOUR

DRUMLANRIG CASTLE

OPPOSITE: *Drumlanrig's oak staircase hall showing the turned banisters and unusual pillar supporting the gallery above. The pictures to the left of the door leading to the morning room are by Murillo, Joost van Cleef and Leonardo da Vinci. The eighteenth-century chinoiserie long-case clock is by Thomas Gordon of Edinburgh.*

LEFT: *The north (entrance) front. Built in 1679–91 on the site of older Douglas castles, Drumlanrig is an unusual combination of French-influenced Baroque and much earlier Scottish castle styles. The splendid horseshoe staircase – inspired by the one at Fontainebleau in France – is unique to Britain.*

THERE CAN BE NO HOUSE IN BRITAIN that better demonstrates the passage of aristocracy from feudal warlords to cultivated patricians than Drumlanrig Castle. Set in the unpopulated hill country of the south Highlands, Drumlanrig was built in the late seventeenth century around a sixteenth-century castle, which may itself have been built on the site of an earlier one. The present castle's Baroque façade, with pedimented windows, roof balustrading and applied Corinthian pilasters, anticipates the Age of Elegance of the next century. The same is true of the elaborate front entrance, with its elegant horseshoe staircase and clock tower. Yet the structure itself – four tall square towers topped by numerous turrets – harks back to more turbulent times, when castles were fortified and noblemen had control of armies as well as of land.

Drumlanrig was the ancient seat of the Douglases, and the present castle was built for Sir William Douglas, 1st Duke of Queensberry, between 1679 and 1691. The identity of the architect is not certain. For a long time it was held to be Sir William Bruce, but there is no record of his having worked at Drumlanrig at the time. The architect was probably either Robert Mylne, the King's Master Mason, or his son-in-law, James Smith.

The Douglas family emblem, which is emblazoned all over Drumlanrig on every kind of surface, derived from a famous episode in Scottish history, involving Robert the Bruce's boon companion, Sir James Douglas (*c.* 1286–1330). Known as the Black Douglas because of his swarthy complexion, he had distinguished himself during the

ABOVE: *The east end of the drawing room, showing one of the two magnificent cabinets originally made for Versailles, c. 1675. Above it hangs a portrait of Charles II. On either side are full-length portraits of James VI and I and his Queen, Anne of Denmark.*

OPPOSITE: *The west end of the drawing room. The cabinet on the right, like the one shown above and below, was presented by Louis XIV to Charles II. He gave them to his natural son, the Duke of Monmouth, whose portrait by Lely hangs above. A Louis XV clock by Leroy stands on a Boulle cabinet containing Meissen porcelain.*

RIGHT: *Detail of the cabinet shown above. Supported by carved wooden figures, the decorative scheme refers to Louis XIV's military victories. It probably came from the Gobelins factory in Paris, which made furnishings for royal residences between 1663 and 1694.*

RIGHT: *The oak-panelled dining room was originally the entrance hall, with access from the courtyard. Above the side table hangs a portrait of Lady Jane Douglas – daughter of the 2nd Duke of Queensberry and wife of the 2nd Duke of Buccleuch – and her sister, Lady Anne, by Sir Godfrey Kneller. Flanking the picture are two of the eight William and Mary two-light silver sconces that are arranged around the room. Made by Arthur Manwaring in 1691, they bear the Queen's cypher and crown.*

border wars with the English by burning towns, levying blackmail, raiding cattle and ransoming prisoners for loot. (The English behaved no differently.) Before King Robert died, in 1329 – after the War of Independence, which would secure Scottish sovereignty against English claims for the next three centuries – he is said to have asked Sir James to carry his heart upon a crusade to the Holy Land and to bury it by the Holy Sepulchre in Jerusalem. Sir James and his trusted band of knights took the silver casket containing the heart to the nearest crusade, against the Moors of Granada. Abandoned by their Spanish comrades, the Scottish knights were massacred. Before succumbing to the Saracen blows, Sir James is said to have thrown the casket into the midst of the enemy, shouting, 'Forward, brave heart!' Thereafter, a crowned and winged heart became the emblem of his descendants, sometimes known as the house of the Black Douglas.

Taking their cue from their illustrious ancestor, the Drumlanrig branch of the Douglas family generally remained close to the Crown. The 1st Duke's grandfather had entertained King James VI and I at the earlier castle on the site, and the 1st Duke himself flourished under the Restoration. As Lord Treasurer he became the most powerful man in Scotland. His son, the 2nd Duke, was an active supporter of the Union and piloted the legislation dissolving the Scottish parliament in 1707.

ABOVE: *Detail of the
serving room, which
contains several portraits
of the Buccleuch household
around 1817 by John
Ainslie. Underneath the
picture of Major Walter
Scott is a lively rendition of
the courier to Henry, Duke
of Buccleuch.*

LEFT: *In the front hall,
the crested fireplace was
skilfully constructed out
of wood to resemble local
stone. The bookcase
contains game books,
registers and reference
works. The chair (part
of a set) dates from the
late seventeenth century.*

The 3rd Duke, though known for his kindness, is even better remembered for his wife, the lovely but spoilt Catherine (Kitty) Hyde, correspondent of Swift and Pope. She never liked Scotland and spent as much time as possible on the family's English estates – as did the 4th Duke. The rents from Drumlanrig were squeezed to finance their lavish lifestyle south of the border. By 1810, when the 4th Duke died, unmarried, the castle was semi-derelict, and all the woods had been cut down.

Fortunately, the Queensberry dukedom (which, like some other Scottish titles, passes through the female line) became joined thereafter with that of Buccleuch, held by the Scott family. The estates of a third dukedom – that of Montagu, which became extinct – were added by marriage, and the family now boasts the rather cumbersome triple-barrelled surname of Montagu-Douglas-Scott. The enormous wealth thus accrued has served Drumlanrig well. Not only has the entire estate undergone a long period of repair and renewal, but, in addition, as other estates were sold, the castle received their paintings, furniture and other treasures. Today, Drumlanrig houses an art collection that includes paintings by Rembrandt, Holbein and Leonardo da Vinci. Yet despite receiving some 30,000 visitors each summer, it preserves the feeling of a lived-in family house to a remarkable degree.

CAIRNESS HOUSE

OPPOSITE: *Looking into the Egyptian room – conceived as the billiard room – from the hall. The design of Cairness House was influenced by French architectural developments of the late eighteenth century. Egyptian themes were particularly fashionable in Paris, and this is thought to have been the first complete Egyptian room in Britain.*

LEFT: *The entrance front of Cairness House, which, according to the architectural historian Prof. David White, is one of the most important neoclassical houses in the British Isles. It was designed for Charles Gordon in 1789 by the Scottish architect James Playfair, who was among the most advanced of his generation but, unlike his famous architect son, William, remains largely unrecognized.*

BUCHAN, SCOTLAND'S NORTH-EASTERN TRIANGLE, which juts into the North Sea between Aberdeen and Elgin, is not immediately appealing. The landscape is mostly flat, consisting of arable farms and forestry planted with the ubiquitous sitka spruce. The best feature is the coast, with long stretches of pale yellow sand, grassy dunes and marshlands teeming with flocks of birds. The beaches are gloriously empty, even in summer. In the 1950s and early 1960s, however, things were different. During the annual 'trade weeks' when the factories and workshops closed, workers from Glasgow and Edinburgh made the north-east beaches their playground. One of the many hotels and guest houses that catered to this trade was Cairness House.

Standing starkly among fields of beet and cabbage, having lost its 'policies' (plantations), Cairness House must have seemed forbidding to many holidaymakers – a cold and draughty mansion five kilometres (three miles) from the sea. Not surprisingly, when Mediterranean package holidays became generally affordable, business declined drastically and the farming family who ran the place eventually decided to sell. The prospects for the Grade A listed house looked bleak indeed. The National Trust for Scotland turned it down: too costly to repair, no endowment, practically no visitors. The best that could be reasonably hoped for was conversion into flats; not the sensitive, historically appropriate variety, but something much more utilitarian that would be bound to wreck the interior, destroying its internal harmonies.

BELOW: *The east side of the entrance hall, which the Millers have restored to Playfair's original colour scheme. An early nineteenth-century convex mirror hangs above an 1830s table. The plaster figurines, which date from c. 1930, are in the neoclassical style. The hall chairs are by Gillow, c. 1790.*

LEFT: *The chimney piece in the Egyptian room showing the hieroglyphs, which are purely decorative. All the chimney pieces and plasterwork moulds at Cairness were made by Richard Rathbone in 1795 and shipped from London the same year.*

OPPOSITE: *The entrance hall viewed from the front door. By continuing the lines of the pilasters across both the marble floor and the ceiling, Playfair created a strong architectural frame, reminiscent of an inner courtyard.*

RIGHT: *The Millers have restored the library to Playfair's original colour scheme. The bookcases and most of the detailing are original, apart from the silk lining in the glass doors, which is modern but is an exact match.*

OPPOSITE: *The* enfilade *of rooms, from the library, through the hall and then the breakfast room, culminating in the dining room. The circle and rectangle theme used in the library is repeated in all the mahogany doors.*

BELOW: *The Millers use this recessed cabinet in the 'business room' to display some of their collection of creamware ceramics, c. 1800.*

Enter a brave and enterprising English couple, Patricia and Philip Miller. Philip is an architect and architectural historian with a passion for neoclassicism and ceramics. Patricia is an interior designer and conservationist. Together they had helped restore Ampthill Park in Bedfordshire, an important William Chambers house. Despite having little money behind them, they wasted no time when they saw the advertisement in *Country Life* and within 48 hours they were viewing the house. Philip had known about Cairness since student days, and seeing it in the flesh was no disappointment. In 1994, throwing caution to the wind, they decided to take it on.

The house owes its existence to Charles Gordon (1749–96), scion of an old Buchan family, who manipulated a series of legacies into a considerable fortune. In 1789, he commissioned the Perthshire-born architect James Playfair, who was then practising in London and was among the most avant-garde members of his profession, to design him a brand-new palace in the bleak reaches of Buchan.

Playfair had recently spent some weeks in Paris, and he incorporated some of the latest French architectural ideas into his plan for Cairness. These were apparent in his adoption of elementary geometric forms – the square, the circle, the semicircle – as can be seen in his two lunette arches (beloved of French neoclassicists), as well as the round icehouse enclosed in a great semicircular office behind the main façade. Playfair died in 1793, before his designs for the interior rooms were executed, and his client scarcely saw their completion before he died in 1796.

Charles Gordon's son, Thomas Gordon, inherited the property at the age of seven. Appropriately for the owner of a neoclassical mansion with Doric (ie, Grecian) motifs, he grew up to become a

passionate philhellene. Trained as an officer in the Royal Scots Greys, he served in the Greek War of Independence. In 1823, 'Greek' Gordon, as he became known, was briefly Chief of Staff in the Greek army. By this time he was a Greek national hero. He returned to Cairness in the late 1820s and died there in 1841, survived by his devoted servant – a huge Greek Armenian known locally as Johnny Turk! Playfair's ambitious project was finally brought to fruition in 1891 by 'Greek' Gordon's grandson, Charles Thomas Gordon, who built the gates and lodges to Playfair's design. Eventually, however, the Gordons were obliged to sell Cairness to a local farmer. During the Second World War, the house was used as offices, before serving as a guest house in the post-war era.

As often happens, it was the relative neglect suffered by Cairness following the departure of the Gordons that also made its salvation possible. The family that owned it did very little beyond applying the odd coat of paint. Remarkably, the library, with its geometrically patterned built-in cupboards, survived unaltered, as did the Egyptian room.

The task of restoration has been slow and painstaking. The Millers are sticklers for authenticity, paying special attention to colours. Furnishings have been improvised, in some cases from junk shops. In summer the drawing room is used for concerts of eighteenth-century music, played on the original instruments. Though the house's future is not yet quite secure, there can be no doubt that the Millers' intervention has saved Cairness House for posterity.

ABOVE: *The dining room has been carefully restored by the Millers to Playfair's original blue and terracotta colour scheme. The table, c. 1830, was bought by the Millers especially for the house. The dinner service is Spode, c. 1810, and the figures bearing the lamps date from the early nineteenth century.*

OPPOSITE: *The upper corridor was decorated by the previous owners in the 1970s. At the far end is the laird's (master's) dressing room. The early nineteenth-century vases are French.*

59

VISIONS
OF SPLENDOUR

HOPETOUN HOUSE

OPPOSITE: *Lit by an octagonal cupola, the staircase stands at the core of the original part of Hopetoun. The walls are lined with pine panelling carved with festoons of fruit and flowers, ears of wheat and peapods by the Scottish woodcarver, Alexander Eizat, who worked with Sir William Bruce at Holyrood. The trompe l'oeil panels were painted in 1967 by the Scottish artist William McLaren.*

LEFT: *The central block of Hopetoun's west front showing the architect Sir William Bruce's original elevation, built between 1699 and 1702. French influence is apparent in the bold semicircular pediment. The balustrades of William Adam's east front, commenced two decades later, can be seen above the roof-line of what was originally intended to be a three-storey rectangular block.*

A FINE PANORAMIC LANDSCAPE, painted by the eighteenth-century Scottish landscape painter Andrew Wilson, now in the private apartments of the Marquess of Linlithgow, shows Hopetoun House viewed from an 'elevated point across the Firth', with sheep in the foreground and shepherds poised, in the Claudian manner, under the shade of what is probably an ilex tree. Interestingly, the artist, who studied in Italy, has taken the liberty of moving the cupolas on each side of William Adam's magnificent façade to a different position.

Today the same view would still show the sheep and house in their idyllic parkland setting, but beyond the Hopetoun estate, much has changed. Distant chimneys spew out chemicals. Aircraft whine their way to nearby Edinburgh airport. Across the Firth the naval dockyards of Rosyth, with terminals and oil drums, stand where Wilson saw only fields and woods and sailing craft. The Lowland Arcadia of Hopetoun is now overlooked by the Forth rail and road bridges – monuments, respectively, to the nineteenth and twentieth centuries. To Adam's credit, his architecture meets the challenge, the horizontal sweep of his façade complementing the bridges' towering structures.

Hopetoun has often been called Scotland's Versailles, a palace standing in acres of landscaped grounds within easy reach of Edinburgh and swarming with summer visitors. But in its present incarnation it is much more than a stop on the tourist trail. Established as a private charitable trust by its owners, the 3rd Marquess of Linlithgow and his son

RIGHT: *The yellow
drawing room in the state
apartments. The yellow
silk damask dates from
1850. The large painting
is* The Adoration of the
Shepherds *from the studio
of Rubens. The portrait of
an old woman reading is by
Salomon Koninck.*

OPPOSITE: *Part of
the* enfilade *of state
apartments created by
William Adam, leading
from the yellow drawing
room through the red
drawing room to the dining
room. The gilt console
table and pier glass are part
of the original eighteenth-
century dining room
furniture designed by
James Cullen.*

BELOW: *A seventeenth-
century Dutch ebonized
painted and gilded side
table, with matching
candle stand, in the west
wainscot bedchamber.*

Adrian (now the 4th Marquess), in 1974, it is protected, in perpetuity, against any decline in family fortunes or the attentions of corporate predators.

The Hopes are descended from a family of Edinburgh burgesses and lawyers whose fortunes prospered during the seventeenth century through a judicious combination of luck and ability. Sir James Hope (1614–61) came into possession, through marriage, of valuable lead mines in Lanarkshire. After studying mineralogy in the Netherlands, he brought the art of mining to a level hitherto unknown in Scotland, enriching himself in the process. The Hopetoun property was bought for his grandson Charles Hope while he was still a minor. The boy's father, John, had bought a nearby estate in 1678 but had met an early death four years later in the shipwreck of the *Royal Gloucester*, a frigate bearing the future James VII and II (then Duke of York). According to family tradition, John Hope gave up his seat in the only lifeboat to the Duke – and his dogs. For this act of loyalty, John's son Charles was made the 1st Earl of Hopetoun on reaching his majority in 1703. Thereafter, as zealous supporters of the Union, his descendants became pillars of the British establishment. The 2nd Earl was one of the Lords of Police; the 4th Earl, who was a general during the Napoleonic wars, supervised the embarkation of the British army after the Battle of Corunna in 1809. The 7th Earl was appointed first Governor General of Australia in 1900 and created Marquess of Linlithgow in 1902. The 2nd Marquess was Viceroy of India from 1936 to 1943.

The palace is really two houses, whose slightly uneasy conjunction reflects the growing ambitions of the 1st Earl of Hopetoun. During his minority, his mother, Lady Margaret, hired Scotland's best-known architect, Sir William Bruce, who had remodelled the royal palace of Holyrood in Edinburgh, to design a house fit for her son.

ABOVE: *The state dining room, decorated in the early nineteenth century by James Gillespie Graham, is a fine example of late Regency style, with most of the furniture dating from 1820. In 1822 George IV visited Hopetoun as the guest of the 4th Earl. This was part of the King's famous visit to Scotland – the first by a reigning monarch since Charles II.*

In keeping with contemporary taste, Bruce designed a Palladian villa, the west half of which, built between 1699 and 1702, remains on the garden side. Beautifully proportioned, it is a model of classical restraint.

Following his elevation to the peerage, however, the building proved too modest for the 1st Earl, and in 1721 he asked William Adam to enlarge and extend it. Adam designed the east façade, with its flanking colonnades and pavilions, as an architectural expression in the grandest manner of the owner's station and influence. The work was not yet fully completed when William Adam died, in 1748; it was left to his sons to finish it. Robert, who was to become the most famous, had worked closely with his father on the project. It is recorded that 'on every consultation of the earl with his friend [William Adam] the young Robert was called on to give his opinion before anything could be decided'.

Impressive as it is, the great Georgian mansion never quite meshes with its predecessor. The east front, as the architectural historian John Fleming has pointed out, succeeds in imposing itself as a unified conception. On the garden side, however, 'the predominantly vertical emphasis of Bruce's original house distinguishes it at once from its later

LEFT: *The bedchamber designed by Sir William Bruce for the young 1st Earl. The gilt four-poster bed, hung with red damask, was brought from London in 1768. The painting over the door is one of a series commissioned in 1703 from the artist Philip Tideman, who was working in Amsterdam. Entitled* The Patronage of Music, *it was intended to give moral encouragement to the room's occupant.*

BELOW: *Boxes in the eighteenth-century charter room, containing title deeds and other legal documents. With its fireproof stone-vaulted ceiling and heavy iron door, the small chamber, which was converted in 1708, gives a good idea of how provision was made to safeguard family papers.*

accretions, and one can but wonder if William Adam did not intend to case it in, or sweep it away altogether'.

This lack of integration, however, lends charm to the interior. After William Adam's death, his sons, John, Robert and James, decorated the new rooms, and these convey a sense of princely magnificence designed to impress. The older, Bruce rooms were left untouched and are, by contrast, cosy and modestly proportioned, with panelled walls typical of the seventeenth century.

Today, Hopetoun's proximity to the Scottish capital means that scarcely a day passes without some function or other taking place in William Adam's magnificent ball-room wing. And because its future is assured, a fascinating composite essay by Scotland's great classical architects has been preserved for posterity.

MOUNT STUART

ABOVE: *The east (garden) front of Mount Stuart. Commissioned by the 3rd Marquess of Bute after a fire destroyed most of the older building in 1877, the new building was designed by the Edinburgh architect Sir Robert Rowand Anderson.*

OPPOSITE: *One side of the four-square gallery overlooking the huge central hall. The bronze railings are copies of those around the tomb of the Emperor Charlemagne at Aachen. The decorated vaulted ceilings are groined with fragrant cedarwood.*

O N DECEMBER 3, 1877, a fire almost destroyed Mount Stuart, a Palladian mansion west of Glasgow on the Isle of Bute, and seat of the Earls and Marquesses of Bute. The 3rd Marquess was in London at the time and learned of the fire by telegram. History does not record his immediate response. But events would show that he saw in this disaster the opportunity to replace the Georgian box he had inherited with a stately pleasure-dome more suited to his taste.

The original mansion had been built for his great-great-great grandfather, the 2nd Earl of Bute, in 1716–19. His son, the 3rd Earl, served as Prime Minister under George III in 1762–3, but he was so unpopular that he had to surround himself with prizefighters to protect him against random attacks by members of the public.

The 3rd Earl's great-grandson, John Patrick Crichton-Stuart, 3rd Marquess of Bute, was born in 1847 with more than the proverbial silver spoon in his mouth. When he

RIGHT: *The horoscope room was originally created as the 3rd Marquess's sitting room. The amazing castellated mirror reflects a section of the decorated ceiling panels and the painted frieze of arches on the opposite wall, echoing Anderson's marble Gothic arches leading to the conservatory.*

OPPOSITE: *Towering 24 metres (80 feet) above the marble hall, the azure vaulted ceiling depicts the constellations. The stars, which are made from silver-backed glass, appear to move with the passage of the sun. The stained-glass windows illustrate the signs of the Zodiac.*

BELOW: *The central panel of the ceiling, encircled by a frieze of miniature castles, shows an exact astrological depiction of the position of the planets at the time of the 3rd Marquess's birth, on September 12, 1847.*

reached his majority he was reputed to be the richest man in Britain, with an annual income of £300,000. His father had married two immensely wealthy heiresses in succession, the first of whom had brought him vast estates in South Wales, particularly in Cardiff, and he had been instrumental in the development of Cardiff as a port.

The 3rd Marquess was romantically and mystically inclined. Inspired by the Catholic Gothicism of the architect and designer A W N Pugin and his followers, he scandalized many of his contemporaries by adopting the Roman faith. His religious and aesthetic ideas were of a piece: it was not the narrow ecclesiasticism of the Church that drew him, but rather the poetic mysticism of the most influential of the nineteenth-century English converts, Cardinal John Henry Newman. Benjamin Disraeli gently satirized the young Lord Bute's spiritual odyssey in his novel *Lothair*.

The rebuilt Mount Stuart, still unfinished inside when the 3rd Marquess died in 1900, is a cathedral of the senses, where colour, light and symbolism combine to give pleasure and spiritual uplift. Here, astrology, paganism and orthodoxy meet under the overarching frame of the neo-Gothic sublime, and paintings of holy martyrs line the same walls as those of the ancestors of the Butes, who claimed descent from the royal House of Stuart. The Marquess's obsession with his lineage blends into the transcendental themes crafted into the fabric of the church-like interior, suggesting that somewhere within his psyche there lodged the ancient Stuart belief in the Divine Right of Kings.

The Marquess had worked with the well-known English neo-Gothic architect William Burges in rebuilding Cardiff Castle in the Gothic style, and he had also designed a small

MOUNT STUART

RIGHT: *In the stained glass windows on the grand marble staircase, the arms of the Earls of Bute (centre), flanked by those of the Pembrokes (right) and the Earls of Dumfries (left), are depicted in a family tree represented by a rose bush. The stained glass and the paintings in the spandrels of the arches illustrating the Days of Creation are by H W Lonsdale. Family portraits hang on the walls.*

OPPOSITE: *Originally
intended as three rooms,
the drawing room is
divided by screens of
marble columns – a device
invented by Robert Adam
but translated into Gothic
by Anderson. The heraldic
ceiling depicts the family
tree and is set against a
ground of polished mica.*

BELOW: *William Frame
was responsible for the
woodwork in the library as
in most of the house,
though it was completed by
Anderson in 1912. Family
portraits adorn the walls.*

chapel at Mount Stuart in 1873. Yet it was to an Edinburgh architect, Sir Robert Rowand
Anderson (who went on to design the Scottish National Portrait Gallery) that he turned
for the design of the new Mount Stuart. Anderson, who had worked under the great
Gothicist Sir Gilbert Scott in London, was a scholarly architect. He had published
learned articles about the Gothic architecture of France and Italy, and the flat wall planes
of the eastern façade of Mount Stuart have a distinctly Venetian feel. Another architect,
William Frame, was hired to decorate most of the interior. He was responsible for the
woodwork and timber ceilings, which were made in the Bute workshops at Cardiff Castle
and shipped to the island by sea. Mount Stuart was kitted out with the latest technological
luxuries. The heated Gothic-style swimming pool in the basement was the first to be fitted
in any private house. In 1883 Mount Stuart became the first house in Scotland to be lit by
electricity. A telephone cable was introduced in 1887. All this probably made a greater
impression than the beautiful stained glass or marbles imported specially from Carrara in
Italy. Lord Bute's friend and biographer, Sir David Hunter Blair, recalled that when he
stayed at Mount Stuart in 1886, what struck him most was to see his hostess 'press a
button by her chair in the drawing room and flood the room instantly with dazzling light'.

Mount Stuart's brilliance was short-lived. The new century saw a fierce reaction against
Victorian Gothic, and the house was neglected for decades. In the 1960s, however, the far-
sighted 6th Marquess undertook a major renovation of the house and grounds with the
aim of 'preserving Mount Stuart House, policies [plantations] and estate as an integral
unit'. With this end, the Mount Stuart Trust was created and is today overseen by the 7th
Marquess, Johnny Dumfries.

VISIONS
OF SPLENDOUR

TYNINGHAME HOUSE

ABOVE: *Tyninghame House, near the north Berwickshire coast, has been owned by the Earls of Haddington for over 350 years.*
In 1829–33 it was remodelled by the architect William Burn to create a castle in the Scots Baronial style.

OPPOSITE: *An eighteenth-century Venetian mirror and a gilt-wood Italian console table*
echo the curves of the original 1830 flock wallpaper, which was carefully cleaned
and patched by paper conservers.

THE CASUAL VISITOR, MEETING TIM CLIFFORD, Director of the National Gallery of Scotland, and his wife, Jane, for the first time in the magnificent surroundings of Tyninghame, a Scots Baronial castle in Berwickshire, might be forgiven for assuming that they are the exclusive occupants. The approach is through a beautiful formal garden. On entering the house, the visitor is quickly enfolded in a large room flooded with light from huge mullioned windows overlooking the gardens and parkland. Packed with furniture and a myriad of fine artefacts that reflect Tim's passion for collecting, the drawing room creates an impression of sumptuous richness. Although none of the other rooms can compete in grandeur with the drawing room, Jane's talent as a design consultant has ensured that all the rooms are decorated with panache. They are crowded with objects arranged as if they had been there for ever.

Tyninghame, however, is not all it seems. It has been owned by the Earls of Haddington for over 350 years, but the present Earl, already settled in the other great

TYNINGHAME HOUSE

RIGHT: *Tim and Jane have gone to great lengths to preserve the 20-metre (65-foot) drawing room as Burn designed it. The exuberant array of furniture, glass, ceramics, sculpture and double-banked pictures on the walls reflects Tim's passion for collecting. The carpet is original to the room and was laid in 1830.*

ABOVE: *Baroque bronzes
are displayed on a Sheraton
table in the drawing room.
A resin reproduction of a
sixteenth-century bronze
horse by the Florentine
sculptor Giambologna
stands atop an inlaid
ebony cabinet.*

OPPOSITE: *In the corridor
adjoining the drawing
room, a mid-eighteenth-
century gilt-wood English
mirror hangs above a
German walnut and parcel-
gilt table displaying Kangxi
(Chinese) blue and white
porcelain. The shell-backed
chairs are Regency.*

family seat, at Mellerstain, near Melrose, felt unable to maintain a second house after he inherited from his father in 1986. Wishing to retain the land on the estate, he explored various options for the house, but all were eventually rejected as impracticable. In 1987, most of the contents of Tyninghame were sold at auction by Sotheby's.

A chance meeting with Kit Martin solved the problem. A specialist in dividing up large mansions, Martin took over the house and 24 hectares (60 acres) in 1987. With the Edinburgh architectural firm Simpson & Brown, he converted it and the surrounding estate buildings into 17 self-contained houses and cottages. Martin undertook to leave the exterior and all the principal rooms unaltered and to maintain the grounds around the house. The Earl gave covenants that the parkland would be left as pasture and the trees and avenues maintained, thus ensuring the continuity of Tyninghame's unspoilt setting.

Martin has a consistent approach to country-house conversions. By making vertical rather than horizontal divisions and retaining the original reception rooms, he creates 'houses within houses', each with its own front entrance at ground level. Not only did Tyninghame divide naturally into vertical segments, but the estate buildings in all their variety provided him with a perfect opportunity to exercise his imagination and skills.

With its turrets, crow-stepped gables and dormers, Tyninghame resembles a pedigree Victorian Scots Baronial mansion. But the Scottish architect William Burn's extensive

ABOVE: *The library on the second floor. The bookcase was copied from one at Hopetoun House. Made of MDF (medium-density fibreboard), it was grained to resemble oak. Over the mantelpiece hangs* A Question of Taste, *an early Victorian painting by the Scottish artist Alexander Fraser. In the foreground is a Victorian Gothic chair in the style of A W N Pugin.*

remodelling from 1829 to 1833, commissioned by the 8th Earl, was, in fact, a reworking of the existing mansion, which had been in the Haddington family since 1623. The estate owes its present appearance largely to the 6th Earl and his wife, Helen, sister of the 1st Earl of Hopetoun, who, in the early eighteenth century, apparently inspired him to plant trees where no one thought they could grow. Like other Unionist peers – including the owners of Drumlanrig and Hopetoun – the 6th Earl took advantage of the commercial opportunities opened up by the parliamentary union with England, creating extensive plantations with fine avenues, and shelter belts for timber.

Tyninghame is a key work in the emergence of the Scots Baronial style, which was later developed to maturity by Burn's partner, David Bryce. Indeed, the pair can claim responsibility for starting the whole movement by commissioning the English antiquarian Robert William Billings to record Scotland's ancient architectural heritage. When in 1852 Billings's *Baronial and Ecclesiastical Antiquities of Scotland* appeared in four volumes,

ABOVE: *The dining room, which is on the ground floor. The curtains are by Laura Ashley, for whom Jane worked as personal artistic adviser. At the far right, in front of a small mirror, stands a bust of Sir Isaac Newton, while a bust of Homer shares the window sill with a classical Apulian vase. The wallpaper is by Zoffany.*

lairds throughout the land seized on them as pattern books, and architects pored over them for ideas. Billings was credited with having rediscovered a legitimate Scottish voice, and it was he who coined the word 'Baronial' to describe what he saw as a distinct national architecture.

Never ponderous, Burn's lightness of touch is demonstrated by his numerous gently tapering candle-snuffer towers and turrets, and the tiny balconies to the tower windows resembling illustrations to Sir Walter Scott's *The Lady of the Lake.* Most impressive of all are his asymmetrical elevations. The extended broken plan of the house, in which doors open out onto each front, made it more feasible for every apartment to have its own front door without the exterior having to be altered. Each of the main conversions was able to incorporate one or two of the first-floor state rooms, providing a living space comparable in size to that of the Cliffords. The solution adopted at Tyninghame offers a model to be emulated in the twenty-first century for houses that are much too large for a single family.

CASTING

ADRIFT

CASTING
ADRIFT

TIREE BLACK-HOUSES

ABOVE: *The settlement of Ruaig, showing the Lairds' cottages, at the far left and right of the photo. The traditional 'black-houses' have massive walls consisting of two layers of stone infilled with sand; the roofs, which were originally thatched, sit on the inner walls so water soaks away through the sand.*

OPPOSITE: *The attic in 'Rachel's House', owned by Kirsty Laird since 1963, was refloored to provide a bedroom cum studio. By the bed is a washed-up balsa-wood stool from the Indian Ocean island of Lamu. A net larder hangs by the window.*

T HERE'S A TRADITION ON TIREE that if a ship comes to grief, once everything has been done to save the crew the wreckage is a gift from the sea. Bottles of alcohol and thousands of packets of cigarettes – alas, only worth the value of their coupons – came ashore in 1972 after the *Loch Seaforth* ferry hit the rocks. But on a treeless island where timber is gold, the greatest 'gift' from the sea is driftwood. This, together with all the other flotsam and jetsam yielded by the ocean, comprises the chief material of artist Kirsty Laird's work. Like the island itself, each of her *objets trouvés* has a timeless quality. The secrets of its origin, age and history belong to the ocean, while corrosion enriches its patina and shape. Fascinated by chance, she sometimes combines two or more objects to create something new, thus completing the process of transformation.

The Lairds first visited the island, the outermost of the Inner Hebrides, on holiday in 1963. Kirsty's late husband, Michael, an architect, was enchanted by the distinctive and strangely modern-looking 'black-houses'. Many were abandoned and crumbling.

CASTING
ADRIFT

TIREE BLACK-HOUSES

RIGHT: *The ground floor consists of one room, with the sitting area at one end and the eating area (shown here) at the other. The kitchen is behind the attic steps. Though the stained pine beams are original, the Lairds were obliged to lay a new cork-tiled floor. A late eighteenth-century Scottish dresser and an old carved oak settle stand between the windows, which face south-west onto the sea. There is no plumbing or electricity.*

ABOVE: *The bedroom in 'Neil's House', named after the previous owner, who sold it to the Lairds in 1967. The corner cabinet, containing Kirsty's model ship collection, is the underneath of a back-to-back ferry seat washed ashore after the* Loch Seaforth *ferry struck rocks in 1972. The wicker ship-fender, by the eighteenth-century Scottish farmhouse chair, is one of three found by Kirsty on the shore.*

Michael determined to rescue one there and then. And so it was that on their first-ever visit they bought 'Rachel's House' for £50. 'Neil's House', a few strides across the grass, was bought four years later.

As its Gaelic name, *Tir-iodh* ('Land of Corn'), suggests, Tiree was once known as the breadbasket of the Inner Hebrides, but it also has a nickname, *Tir fo Thuinn* ('Land Below the Waves'), as it is so flat. When Samuel Johnson visited the island in 1773, he commented that it was notable for its fertility. In the first half of the nineteenth century, the population doubled to around 5,000. But the potato famine of 1846, followed by typhus and cholera, and the decline of the once profitable kelp industry, halved the population. Further depletion resulted from the policy of the landlords, the Dukes of Argyll, who encouraged the islanders to emigrate to Canada with assisted passages.

Nowadays there are about 800 people living on Tiree. The sunniest and windiest of the Scottish isles, it attracts windsurfers from all over the world. But for Kirsty Laird it is the beaches above all that make the island special – with the treasures they bring from the sea.

RIGHT: *The alabaster ship, probably from Crete, was given to the Lairds' son when he was small by a Tiree seaman. The matchstick model of* The Great Michael, *the biggest Scottish warship of the seventeenth century, was a gift for Michael Laird from friends.*

BELOW: *Propped on the mantelpiece in the kitchen at 'Neil's House' is Kirsty Laird's 'Locked in the Past' – an assemblage of keyholes, locks and bolts taken from pieces of wood and furniture washed ashore. The weathering heightens their mystery.*

CASTING
ADRIFT

ORKNEY CROFT

ABOVE: *Hosan, showing the renovated dwelling area and the byre (cowshed). A typical nineteenth-century interlinking long-house and steading (farmhouse), it is derived from a much older type of croft in use before the agrarian improvements of the eighteenth century.*

OPPOSITE: *View from the living room into the passage leading to the byre. The owners, Peter and Arlene McLaren, intend to convert the byre, barn and hayloft into a studio and study.*

FOR AN ORCADIAN, the 'Mainland' means the largest of the Orkney Islands, rather than the rest of Scotland, and it was there that Arlene Isbister and Peter McLaren bought for a song the abandoned nineteenth-century long-house on the knoll. As well as being successful artists, Peter and Arlene are dedicated Orcadians. Hosan became their joint creative project: a means of combining their skills and developing a better understanding of the craftsmen and masons of earlier times. The tradition of the artisan-builder in Orkney has an ancient lineage. The same flagstones that were used on floors, walls and roofs by the builders of Hosan in the nineteenth century were used in the Stone Age settlement of nearby Skara Brae 5,000 years earlier. Hosan also features an internal door-locking mechanism remarkably similar to one preserved at Skara Brae.

The croft held a family connection. Arlene's great-grandparents had bought Hosan in the 1920s and it remained in the family until, in the 1970s, it was let to what evolved into a commune – the 'Hosan Hippies'. Arlene's great-aunt Maggie, a shepherdess, had worked the croft until 1969. A large, merry lady, she would cut a few peats every year to

BELOW: *In the kitchen–living room, salvaged shutters, floorboards and zinc were combined to make a cupboard. The stone sink until recently served as a water trough for cows.*

RIGHT: *The bedroom leading off the living room showing the surprisingly large 'breast-stone' above the fireplace. The brass bed was bought from a local auction covered in verdigris and black paint, and the Durham quilt came from Kirkwall. One of Arlene's paintings hangs by the bookcase to the right of the window.*

ensure Hosan's peat-rights – something Peter and Arlene thank her for, when they sit in front of their blazing peat fire. The name of the house is derived from the old Norse word *hauss* , meaning 'skull'. For Peter and Arlene it seemed particularly apposite when, digging around the foundations, they found dozens of buried cattle skulls. However, these turned out to be no more than evidence of Maggie's passion for brawn.

Reconstructing the roof was the biggest challenge. The original grey slates had been blown off in a storm in 1953 and replaced with asbestos. Guided by the few traditional craftsmen left in the parish, Peter and Arlene worked out that they needed around 6,000 slates – which had to be salvaged as there were no longer any working quarries left in

ORKNEY CROFT

LEFT: *The flagstone floor of the kitchen–living room, made from local hand-quarried stone, has a polished, marble-like surface created by over a century of wear. In order to lay essential drains, Peter and Arlene had to lift and re-lay the flagstones. Most of the furniture and kitchen equipment were bought at monthly auctions held locally. The upright Orkney chair, made of driftwood with a wicker back, was designed to keep out draughts. On the mantelpiece are two Scottish spongewear bowls.*

Orkney. An advertisement in the local paper took them to the North Isles in a freezing blizzard, riding on tractor and trailer.

The continuity between Orkney's ancient history and the present has influenced Arlene's development as an artist. Interested in man's dislocation from nature, she tries to recover, through the process of painting, a connection with the natural elements. Since moving to Hosan in 1992, Peter has produced a series of effervescent seascapes which, while acknowledging the Scottish landscape tradition, have gone beyond this. Together Peter and Arlene have formed Art Discovery, an educational trust that provides workshops for local children, making them aware of their Orcadian artistic heritage.

CASTING
ADRIFT

CAMASUNARY

OPPOSITE: *The hall at Camasunary fishing lodge, leading into the sitting room. Paper cut-outs of sea trout pasted on the walls preserve memories of angling triumphs and the candlelit suppers that followed. According to Johnson family custom, guests who caught large fish were obliged to make their own replicas using watercolours.*

LEFT: *Camasunary, which can only be reached after a two-hour trek from the nearest road, was converted into a fishing lodge in the early 1900s. The small bothy (hut or cottage) in the distance has been made available to hill walkers as an overnight shelter. There has been a settlement at Camasunary since the early seventeenth century.*

THE ISLE OF SKYE, a flamboyant extrusion of sealochs and peninsulas that spreads out like a hand from the north-west coast of Scotland, contains an astonishing variety of dramatic landscapes, from the ridges and cliffs of Trotternish to the flat-topped peaks of Duirnish known as MacLeod's Tables. The most impressive of its mountains are the Black Cuillins, a range of jagged peaks commanding the south-western skyline. With some twenty 'Munros' – hills of 915 metres (3,000 feet) or more – the Black Cuillins are not for casual strollers. Sudden mists and squalls apparently descend out of nowhere on even the brightest of summer days.

Many a hill walker, thirsty and footsore, must have gazed with longing at Camasunary fishing lodge, set on a beautiful sandy bay locked beneath the Black Cuillins. A private dwelling belonging to the Johnson family, owners of the Camasunary estate since 1915, it is inaccessible by road. The lodge's *raison d'être* has always been the fast-flowing burn (small stream), nursery to many generations of sea trout, that meanders through the flat green pastures lying between the mountains and the shore.

Aware of the scepticism with which merely verbal accounts of fishing prowess are universally greeted, the Johnsons adopted, from 1939, the apparently unique custom of recording every 'moonie' caught by the family or their guests. A 'moonie' was the 'once-in-a-blue-moon' fish that tipped the scales over 3.5 kilograms (8 pounds) – the trout-fishing equivalent of the Munro. Everyone who caught a moonie was duty-bound to paint a picture of it which was cut out and pasted on the walls. One guest who dared to subcontract his duty to a more artistically gifted friend is still remembered with disdain.

The effect of these trophies plastered over the walls is somewhat surreal. The visitor exhausted by the two-hour walk over the pass from the nearest point on the road, or disoriented by an over-generous dram of single malt, might think themselves in an aquarium, or in the fish section of some Victorian museum. Sadly, the latter impression may not be entirely false, as the fish have dwindled drastically. Not a single moonie has been caught at Camasunary since 1985. The dramatic decline in sea trout and wild salmon stocks throughout the west of Scotland has been attributed to environmental pollution and to diseases caught from the salmon farms that litter the coastline, with their attendant gulls. Supermarket salmon may be cheap and nourishing and the farms an important source of employment, but the cost has been high. The painted replicas that are preserved at Camasunary may soon be the only evidence of what used to be one of the finest products of nature's larder.

ABOVE: *A shoal of sea trout curving around the stairwell enticingly points the way to the hall and kitchen.*

RIGHT: *Meals are taken in the living room. Everything at the lodge has to be brought by foot, or by a dump-truck that proceeds over the rough mountain track at a snail's pace.*

OPPOSITE: *Staying at the lodge is a throwback to Victorian living, before electricity and running water became standard. This guest bedroom makes no concessions to modern creature comforts.*

CROVIE COTTAGES

OPPOSITE: *At No. 49, Crovie, a 1953 coronation mug enjoys pride of place on the living room mantelpiece. 1953 was the year that a high tide and gale-force wind forced the residents to abandon their homes. The present owner, Joan Rennie, a retired biology teacher, is one of the few permanent residents at Crovie today.*

LEFT: *Crovie, looking east. Threatened with demolition in the 1950s, Crovie is now recognized as one of the finest eighteenth-century fishing villages in Europe. Most of the houses are listed buildings, and the villagers have formed a preservation society to guard against inappropriate development.*

THE HOUSES IN CROVIE, on the Moray coast east of Banff, cluster precariously under grassy sandstone cliffs like a brood of chicks beneath their mother. The ledge on which they stand is so narrow that visitors' cars must be left halfway down the precipitous road leading to the village with its single, slippery pathway. Many of the houses have their gable ends pointing seawards, like boats, to protect them from the gales and tides that regularly lash the sea wall. Goods and shopping have to be unloaded and taken to the houses by foot or handcart. Far from deterring the village's current residents, wrestling with the shopping in a force-nine gale is part of the attraction. The incomers who rescued the village after its original inhabitants abandoned it relish the sudden contrasts between violence and calm.

Although there was a settlement of fisherfolk at Crovie from the 1720s, most of the village was built in the mid-eighteenth century by Highlanders displaced by the aftermath of the failed Jacobite uprising of 1745. Tough and resourceful, the Highlanders transformed themselves into fisherfolk, catching haddock, mackerel and whiting, and the 'silver darlings' – herring – that once brought prosperity to the North Sea ports. By the 1890s, the village boasted more than 50 vessels. The fish were caught using 'great lines' with hundreds of hooks baited with shellfish gathered by the women.

The advent of drift nets early in the twentieth century put the Crovie fishermen at a disadvantage, as their jetty was too small for the larger boats this innovative method

CASTING ADRIFT

CROVIE COTTAGES

BELOW: *The interior of No. 57. The house was bought in the 1960s from the last remaining daughter of a fishing family, by artist Katrine Graham-Yooll, in an 'act of defiance' against the local council's plan to abandon the village. On the left is one of her drawings.*

LEFT: *The sitting room at No. 14, which belongs to Brian and Fiona Anderson. The cottage retains many of its eighteenth-century features including the original doors and tongue-and-groove ceiling. The present arrangement dates from the 1960s, after the box bed had been removed to increase the amount of space in the room.*

required. By the end of the Second World War most of the men were obliged to fish from the port of Gardenstown, a little way down the coast towards Banff. The *coup de grâce* came in January 1953, when the sea wall was breached by an extra-high tide combined with a massively powerful gale, known locally as the 'big breeze'. The people were forced to leave their houses and take refuge elsewhere. After surveying the damage, the local council decided that many of the houses were beyond repair, and even suggested bulldozing them into the sea. The people were offered council houses in Gardenstown, and many of them accepted. For several years the Crovie houses languished without roofs, crumbling and abandoned.

Fortunately, a number of artists, teachers and other adventurous souls began buying up the derelict houses and restoring them. For some it was a chance of obtaining cheap housing: around 1960, a Crovie cottage could be had for as little as £12. For others it provided the opportunity for an unusual holiday home or weekend retreat. By the 1980s, a thriving community had come into being. A few of these hardy incomers have now become permanent residents, but most are weekenders or summer residents. They are attracted by the beautiful setting with views of the Cromarty coast, the lobster fishing, the lively weekend social life or the opportunity, as one put it, just 'to sit and stare at the sea'.

BELOW: *A Victorian Sunderland lustreware jug stands on a stripped pine chest of drawers in front of the box bed at No. 57. Built-in beds similar to this one in the former kitchen-living room were at one time standard. Most were replaced by bedrooms in attics that had formerly been used for storage and fishermen's tackle.*

THE SQUARE, ROSHVEN

OPPOSITE: *The sitting room viewed from the kitchen through the entrance hall, showing the tongue-and-groove panelling which has been fully restored along with the original partitions.*

LEFT: *The Square, Roshven, built at the beginning of the twentieth century, is one of the earliest concrete buildings in Europe. Fully restored to its original state, it enjoys a secluded setting at the edge of the Roshven estate, a remote district in the western Highlands.*

ROSHVEN, ON THE SOUND OF ARISAIG, west of Fort William, has a quiet beauty that excels even by western Highlands standards. Its shores are luminous with sandy white beaches. The islets that cluster in its bays and estuaries are deliciously inviting. The fingers that push into the sea opposite the craggy silhouettes of the isles of Rum and Muck are covered with weather-beaten oaks. Long preserved by official neglect, Roshven did not have electricity till the 1980s. The first paved road appeared in the 1960s. Before that, most visitors arrived by boat, unpacking their belongings into small boats from the steamers that plied between Glasgow and Tobermory on Mull. The remainder trekked along a pony track too rough for wheeled traffic.

The Square's rather odd-sounding name derives from the fact that it is one of the earliest examples in Europe of a house made from reinforced concrete. The Roshven estate, renowned as one of the loveliest in the western Highlands, was acquired in the 1850s by Hugh and Jemima Blackburn, both of whom made their mark in Victorian Scotland. Hugh, professor of mathematics at Glasgow University, is remembered as the inventor of the Blackburn Pendulum, a device which facilitated several advances in physics. Jemima, who counted the painter and art critic John Ruskin and the novelist Anthony Trollope among her friends, was a talented watercolourist best known for her studies of birds. Indeed, one of the reasons the couple decided to buy the Roshven estate on Hugh's retirement was the richness and variety of the bird life.

THE SQUARE,
ROSHVEN

RIGHT: *The restored kitchen. Previous owners had chipped off most of the panelling and removed internal partitions to create an open-plan living space wholly out of keeping with the original design.*

OPPOSITE: *The guest bedroom has a Victorian iron bedstead, with a Bulgarian icon hanging above it. The narrow pinewood panelling used throughout the cottage creates a sense of spatial continuity.*

BELOW: *An old desk in the sitting room is enlivened by a collection of seashells set in turquoise pigeonholes. The portrait of the old lady reading was painted by the owner's grandmother.*

The cottage was a spin-off from one of the last great feats of Victorian engineering – the Glenfinnan viaduct on the West Highland Railway between Fort William and Mallaig, which passes near the estate. Opened in 1901, the railway still carries steam trains, among the last in regular service in Great Britain. At the time of its construction the viaduct contained the largest concentration in the world of a brand-new building material, reinforced concrete. Impressed by its properties, Hugh Blackburn decided to build a concrete cottage for his grieve (farm manager). The new construction boasted straight, shiny exterior walls, instead of the rough stone rubble normally used for cottages at that time. The grieve was apparently unimpressed, realizing that the new cottage would be damp because of the condensation, and he remained in his old stone house. The Square changed hands several times and suffered through a series of unfortunate modernizations. Paintwork was stripped and interior panelling removed along with internal partitions to create an open-plan living space with a hideous 'rancho-style' fireplace.

In the 1990s, an enterprising Edinburgh couple restored The Square, using it as a weekend retreat for themselves and their family of three grown-up children. Paying strict attention to detail and authenticity, they carefully restored the cottage to its original condition. On the exterior the step gables at each end of the structure, along with the gabled dormers, were restored. Inside, central heating was installed to defeat the condensation that had worried the grieve. Pine tongue-and-groove panelling, typical of Scottish cottages, was added to give extra warmth and then painted in pastel shades that reflect the ever-changing hues of the western Highland light.

ORIGINALS

ARTHUR LODGE

OPPOSITE: *View of the drawing room, which leads off the atrium. The coffered ceiling is based on the design of the Parthenon gates in Athens. The fireplace echoes the design of the entrance porch that the architect, Thomas Hamilton, had already used at Edinburgh's Royal High School.*

LEFT: *Arthur Lodge, completed in 1830, seen here from the south-facing garden side. It was unusual for an Edinburgh house to be built in the Greek Revival style rather than the more typical Georgian. The façade, though highly architectural, does not reflect its scale inside.*

APPROACHING ARTHUR LODGE FROM EDINBURGH city centre along Dalkeith Road gives no hint of the surprises and visual delights in store. But as soon as the door in the grey stone wall facing the busy main street is opened, a glimpse of the interior reveals it to be one of Edinburgh's best-kept secrets.

With its painted dome and mirrored cornice, the entrance hall dazzles with the complexity of its multiple reflections. An enclosed barrel-vaulted marble staircase opens up dramatically into a large atrium, bathed in sunshine from the glazed top-light. With a heavy arcade in front of the stairs and a screen of two Ionic columns in the manner of Robert Adam's ante-room at Syon House in London, the effect is distinctly theatrical and grand. The spacious central atrium is a clear reference to the houses of classical antiquity from which the neoclassicists took inspiration. The plan is unexpectedly deep – almost square – and because the ground falls away to the sides there is a full, light basement.

The area had been developed from 1806 by the Bell family, who owned the surrounding Newington estate. In 1825, George Bell commissioned further plans, which included the site on which Arthur Lodge now stands. Conceived as Scotland's first villa development – probably based on the model of Nash's Regent's Park Village in London – it was intended to realize 'the desire for a house like a country gentleman, but more modest and closer to the life of the town'. Every house in the development was to have its own garden, with shared avenues, porters' lodges and gates.

URBANE
ORIGINALS

ARTHUR LODGE

RIGHT: *Another view
of the drawing room,
showing the full-height
curved window, with its
original 1830 window
seat with knotted fringe.
Whether intentional or
not, the carved Ionic
columns supporting
the seat are turned
upside down.*

LEFT: *The 'state bedroom',
decorated and furnished by
the previous owner, Jack
Howells, in the Napoleonic
style. The mural of
Edinburgh in the 1830s
was painted by Alisdair
Mcleod in 1985. Thomas
Hamilton's masterpiece,
the Royal High School,
can be seen between
the* trompe-l'oeil *Ionic
columns. Over it flies the
Scottish flag, suggesting
the National Assembly in
session. The Empire bed is
raised on a carpeted dais.*

The site was bought by a builder, Robert Mason, who also built the house. Although there is no hard evidence to prove it, experts are agreed that the architect was Thomas Hamilton, Edinburgh's City Architect. He dreamed of designing Grecian-style palaces, and contributed to the city's image as 'The Athens of the North'. The neo-Grecian Royal High School (temporary home to the Scottish Parliament from 1999 to 2001) on Calton Hill was designed by him in 1825. The extravagance of Hamilton's perfectionism created financial havoc for both clients. By 1830 Mason declared himself bankrupt with a long list of creditors. The house was bought by the City Treasurer, David Cunningham, who knew Hamilton; in fact, Cunningham may have had the house specifically designed for his own occupation in the first place. It was quite usual in those days for a builder to build for someone else at his own expense. Among his other undertakings, Cunningham would have overseen the finances of Hamilton's architectural commissions in the city and clearly it would have been in the architect's interests to please him.

Arthur Lodge was a *tour de force*. Although Hamilton had never travelled to Greece, he was an eager student of Stuart and Revett's *The Antiquities of Athens*. The garden façade, composed of single-storey side wings, a porch and a two-storey pedimented central block, is a perfect essay in the Greek Revival style. The attention to the masonry

ABOVE: *Nothing survives of the original decoration in the dining room, which was imaginatively reinterpreted by the previous owners in 1985. Salvaged Ionic columns were stripped and marbled to match the 'rouge royale' marble chimney piece. The cast cornice frieze came from an original section at Dunmore Park in Perthshire. Eighteenth-century engravings stand out against the grey walls, and neoclassical figurines (after Canova) adorn the side table.*

detailing, which is beautifully pointed and incised with anthemions (a classical motif resembling honeysuckle), is impeccable. In the inner hall, such is the perfection of the masonry that the stone flags on the floor turn imperceptibly upwards to meet the base of each column. Hamilton considered that the height of a room should vary according to its other dimensions, so no two rooms in any part of the house have the same ceiling height.

In 1985, Arthur Lodge was restored by its then owners, Jack Howells, a conservationist, and the barrister John Pinkerton, QC. Wishing to remain faithful to the house's

RIGHT: *Now the entrance hall, this room was altered and embellished in 1899 by the then owners, the Usher family. The painted dome ceiling and the mirrored cornice are clearly indebted to the English neoclassical architect Sir John Soane.*

OPPOSITE: *Looking down the arched marble staircase to the entrance hall. Beyond the screen is an entrance lobby, in the form of a mini-conservatory, which opens onto the street. The passage-like staircase has a barrel-vaulted and coffered ceiling and wooden panelling on the walls.*

very individual design while at the same time creating a comfortable home, they installed a kitchen in one of the bedrooms leading off the atrium, and renovated the other in the Napoleonic style to startling effect, with murals of Edinburgh in the 1830s. The present owner, Roland Friden, is at pains to keep everything much the same. The room he likes best is the Octagon, named for its shape. Leading off from the upstairs landing, it is small and the most perfectly preserved room in the house, providing an occasionally welcome relief from the flamboyance downstairs. From its balcony overlooking the delightful garden, there are views of Craigmillar Castle, the Pentland Hills and, appropriately, the craggy shoulder of Arthur's Seat.

ATHOLL CRESCENT

OPPOSITE: *A moose gazes balefully over the elegant stairwell at No. 9 Atholl Crescent. Beneath it, on an 1820s mahogany sideboard, stands a pair of ospreys by Victorian naturalist and master taxidermist Rowland Ward.*

LEFT: *The Regency curve of Atholl Crescent, under the tower of the Church of St George's West. The Crescent, part of the West End extension of Edinburgh's New Town developed in the 1820s, was designed by Thomas Bonnar.*

AN UNSUSPECTING PEDESTRIAN strolling along Atholl Crescent, an elegant Regency extension of Edinburgh's New Town, may well have their stride arrested by something strange in the front window of No. 9. There may be a toucan skeleton, with massive curved bill improbably supported by an exquisite arrangement of tiny bones; a pair of dancing lizards, with rakish grins; or a sweet little dog which takes an unconscionably long time to disclose that it is stuffed. Further investigation will reveal that the house is actually an antique shop specializing in taxidermy.

Edinburgh is the city of Robert Louis Stevenson, author of *The Strange Case of Dr Jekyll and Mr Hyde*. It is also the city of Burke and Hare, the murderous pair who made headlines at their trial in 1829 (the very time when Atholl Crescent was being constructed) for smothering their lodgers and selling their corpses for dissection. Scotland's capital is certainly not averse to the macabre. Nevertheless, the person who ventures to ring the doorbell of No. 9 is in for a big surprise.

Emma Hawkins is a bright and personable young Australian – the very antithesis of the sinister Hitchcockian figure one might associate with stuffed animals. After serving her apprenticeship in silver and jewellery, she opted for taxidermy. She thinks this was partly because her father, who is now her business partner, gave her real stuffed animals instead of the ersatz cuddly variety when she was little. A giraffe's head on the nursery wall made a lasting impression, becoming the object of enduring love.

ATHOLL CRESCENT

RIGHT: *A rare collection of birds, including a crowned crane and white egret, mounted by Rowland Ward c. 1890, stands on a French console table, throwing exotic shadows on the wall.*

BELOW: *A trumpeter swan preens itself above an 1840s wheelchair. Several of these chairs are distributed around the house. They are perfect for parties as they can be moved around with a minimum of fuss.*

RIGHT: *The mantelpiece in an upstairs drawing room supports six glass display cabinets containing ornamental feathers which came from a 1920s milliner's shop. The nineteenth-century clock is by Bryson of Edinburgh. Two 'rocking crocs', which have been arranged anthropomorphically to display satchels and schoolboy grins, stand on a case of tropical birds mounted by Rowland Ward. The display cabinet to the left of the fireplace contains an assortment of esoteric items, including an engraved emu's egg, a lacquered frog and an engine-turned teapot. At the top of the cabinet is a rare example of a woolly monkey, which has also been mounted by Rowland Ward.*

Emma does not see the animals as sinister but admires them as objects both scientific and beautiful. Not only has she attained an eminent position in the niche market, but her fascination with a craft once associated only with fusty Victorian museums is thoroughly in tune with modern sensibilities. With artists such as Rebecca Horn and Damien Hirst drawing the crowds in with kinetic feathered machines or pickled sheep, Emma's menagerie chimes in well with the contemporary zeitgeist.

Emma and her father bought the house on a visit to Edinburgh for a family wedding. Like the other houses in the Crescent, it had been used for offices, but it is the only one that has been restored to its original condition and is still in private hands. Emma was attracted by the clean lines and functional simplicity of the interiors. An empathy for at least one of the previous occupants may also have played its part. During the 1840s, the prolific writer and publisher Robert Chambers, editor of the *Chambers Encyclopaedia* and one of the precursors of Charles Darwin, lived at No. 9. While resident here, he wrote his famous *Vestiges of the Natural History of Creation*, published 15 years before Darwin's *Origin of the Species*.

Today, with so many species on the verge of extinction, Emma regards taxidermy as a form of conservation. 'In far too many cases,' she says, 'the only specimens left are the ones we now see in cabinets.'

RIGHT: *A stuffed anteater and a toucan skeleton survey the dining room table from the sideboard. Next to the sideboard stands a fibreglass replica of a dodo. The only preserved specimens of the flightless bird, which became extinct in the eighteenth century, were destroyed by fire.*

BELOW: *A set of Scottish crested-back chairs lends gravitas to the kitchen table, which is actually a Regency serving table similar to one in the Brighton Pavilion. The walls are adorned with various maritime trophies, including giant turtle shells, swordfish skulls and salmon. A Scottish medical cabinet is mounted above the side table on the right.*

CLIFTON HOUSE

OPPOSITE: *A trio of gilded and painted Florentine cherubs in carved wood welcomes guests in the hall at Clifton House, above a mirror reflecting early nineteenth-century hand-blocked 'Beckford' wallpaper by Coles of London. The engraving of dogs' heads is by the Victorian artists Edwin and Thomas Landseer. Above it, the fan paper is from the French Revolution.*

LEFT: *Clifton House from the street, with Virginia creeper entirely covering the walls. Built in 1874 when Nairn was first developed as a seaside and golfing resort, the house has been in Gordon Macintyre's family for more than 60 years. Today it is run as a small family hotel and also holds a licence as a theatre.*

AIRN ON THE MORAY FIRTH is close to the site of Culloden, where the Highland clans who supported Bonnie Prince Charlie met their doom in 1745. But despite being situated on the edge of the Highlands, it has a decidedly Lowland ambience. It began its life as a mixed village of Gaelic-speaking fishermen and English-speaking farmers, enabling James VI to boast that one of the towns in his kingdom was so large that people at one end of the main street could not understand those at the other end. Nairn's main expansion occurred in the nineteenth century when the railway brought its sandy beaches within reach of wealthy city folk and retired Empire builders. They constructed spacious villas to enjoy the magnificent views of the Ross-shire and Sutherland hills across the Firth.

Subsequently converted to guest houses, many villas now cater for serious golfers and well-drilled families who reward themselves for goose-pimpled days on the beach with starchy high teas. Indeed, golfing at Nairn – as elsewhere in eastern Scotland, where the game originated – is no simple leisure activity intended for pleasure. An American golfing correspondent, used to the manicured greens and lavish facilities of Florida, dismissed the clubhouse at Nairn as 'a carport with windows'. 'In Scotland,' he commented acidly, 'they come to golf, not sit around in a plush clubhouse. And at Nairn, if the predominant easterlies are blowing, the first five holes along the beach can be a death march.'

ABOVE: *The flamboyant tone of the main drawing room is set by the hand-blocked Coles wallpaper of stylized pomegranate pattern originally designed by Augustus Pugin and used in the Robing Room and Royal Gallery in London's Palace of Westminster. The brocade on the chairs was rewoven in the 1970s to the original 1849 design by Warners.*

RIGHT: *Three lustre pots by Alan Craiger-Smith, Gordon Macintyre's wife, Muriel, and James Campbell stand in a niche with old claret bottles found in the attic. Muriel Macintyre used to have a pottery at Clifton House but has now turned her skills to making violins.*

Golf and swimming, like much else in Scotland, are subject to the Knox Syndrome, also known as 'Knoxplex'. This condition, which afflicts mainly Lowlanders, is the gloomy legacy of the fiery Reformation preacher John Knox, whose name will be for ever linked with the Puritan revolution in Scotland. The Knoxplex has been identified by Dr Anne Smith as being 'at the root of all of our major national afflictions, from tooth decay to alcoholism'. Its chief symptom is 'a distrust of pleasure so profound as often to be mistaken for religious paranoia'.

In seemingly strait-laced Nairn, Clifton House, built in 1872, is an unexpected delight. An oasis of luxury with a hint of Naughty Nineties' decadence, it is more redolent of *fin de siècle* Paris than of Victorian gentility. The moment one enters the front door, the voluptuous clutter of the house exerts a benign influence, keeping the Knoxplex at bay, if not banishing it altogether.

Clifton House has been owned by the Macintyre family for more than 60 years. Its present incumbents, Gordon and Muriel Macintyre are at pains to make their guests feel at home. Gordon, a witty and charming gentleman of the old school, plays several roles by day – as manager, chef and gardener – while receiving his guests in the evening kitted

LEFT: *The 'green room',
the smaller of two dining
rooms. The same hand-
blocked Coles wallpaper
was used in the film
version of John Fowles's
novel* The French
Lieutenant's Woman. *The
sideboard, dating from
the third quarter of the
nineteenth century, was
part of the original
furnishings of the house.*

BELOW: *Lavishly furnished
with a large four-poster,
this bedroom creates an
atmosphere conducive to
romance. The en suite
bathrooms have been
cunningly crafted to fit the
available spaces.*

out in full Highland costume, complete with kilt and sporran. He is adamant that Nairn is a Highland, not a Lowland, town and this is borne out by Samuel Johnson, who wrote, 'At Nairn we may fix the verge of the Highlands; for here I first saw peat fires, and first heard the Erse [Highland Gaelic] language.' Certainly, it is genuine Highland dash (not the ersatz variety with tartan curtains and antlers) that governs the interior of the house.

Clifton House is the backdrop to an engaging fantasy world where hotel guests are treated as members of a jolly country house party. The wine-list itself is a living refutation of any Knoxish idea that a drink or three must be punished with a hangover. With everything taken a stage beyond the ordinary, it comes as no surprise that the obligatory after-dinner charades played in grand Highland houses such as Balmoral have been upgraded at Clifton to fully fledged theatrical productions. During the winter months, when all but the hardiest golfers will find the links unendurable, the larger of two dining rooms converts into a theatre for concerts, operas and plays, and local Thespians muster like the clansmen of yore. Their campaign is aimed at driving away Calvinist gloom with Highland wit.

KIRKWALL TOWN HOUSE

OPPOSITE: *A Victorian brass chandelier hangs above the arch on the third-floor landing of No. 2 Broad Street, Kirkwall, revealing the simple, elegant proportions of this eighteenth-century Orkney town house. Though the house was derelict for years, few alterations were required to restore the upstairs rooms to their original shape.*

LEFT: *An alleyway in Kirkwall with Broad Street at the end. No. 2, the eighteenth-century house by the telephone kiosk, was built as a tollbooth. Today, the upper floors have been restored for domestic use.*

'ORKNEY LAY ATHWART A GREAT SEA-WAY / from Viking times onwards, and its lore / is crowded with sailors, merchants, adventurers, pilgrims, smugglers, storms and sea-changes. / The shores are strewn with wrack, jetsam, / occasional treasure.' So wrote the late Orcadian poet George Mackay Brown in a verse that encapsulates the islands' distinctive culture. Orkney is not quite a nation, but with a history of human settlement of at least 5,000 years it is much more than an appendage of mainland Scotland. St Magnus Cathedral, founded almost nine centuries ago, lends a gravitas to Kirkwall unmatched by other island cities. The town may be small, but the word 'provincial' does not spring to mind. Its glistening, windswept streets, narrow alleyways and pedestrian-friendly precincts signal something rarer and more special: a metropolis in miniature.

The house at No. 2 Broad Street has had a chequered history. A large sycamore growing from one of the chimneys was host to generations of rooks, whose discarded nests completely blocked the flues, allowing the rainwater to soak through the walls. When Liz Thomson and her family bought the house, in the late 1980s, the upper part had been empty for two years. The downstairs room had been taken over by a grocery, with the stairs narrowed to make way for the marble-topped counters. Before that it had been a men's club. A doctor had lived upstairs in the 1930s, installing patterned glass on

URBANE
ORIGINALS

KIRKWALL TOWN
HOUSE

RIGHT: *Willow-pattern platters are displayed above a wooden Adam-style fire surround installed to replace an unsightly tiled fireplace. During the nineteenth century, the window recesses were used as cupboards. In the foreground are glass fishing floats.*

BELOW: *An 1860 'penny-farthing' bicycle of French design stands next to a Victorian oval table with carved spiral legs, and a collection of oddments such as minerals. The painted chest under the table was used for storing sails.*

LEFT: *Oil lamps in the dining room hang next to a Victorian chain clock, with* faux *bamboo chairs below. The c. 1960 glass-and-chrome trolley on which the glasses are standing is displayed to advantage in this room, showing that eclecticism works well in an elegant setting.*

BELOW: *A Victorian child's locomotive points the way into the attic which houses a rare collection of childhood memorabilia, including prams, cradles, a high chair and toys. The doll in the foreground is German.*

the second floor for privacy. Prior to the doctor's arrival, it had been tea rooms, with a hostel for children from the outlying islands attending Kirkwall Grammar School. In the distant past the house had been the town hall and courthouse, with a makeshift prison in the backyard. It had begun its life, two and a half centuries ago, as a tollbooth.

It took the Thomsons half a day to clear the chimneys, after which the house began to dry out. The rooks were devastated and for years continued to circle the chimneys in anguished despair. A local master-craftsman restored two windows that had been blocked up and converted into cupboards; tiles were removed from some of the fireplaces and replaced with mantelpieces. Otherwise, remarkably little needed doing. Apart from the stairs, which give no hint of the spaciousness above, the eighteenth-century house has remained largely unaltered.

Liz Thomson comes from an old Orcadian family, the Bews. Having spent much of her life in the South, she now returns to Kirkwall every summer. Liz worked for a time in the antiques trade and is an inveterate collector, with an unerring eye for interesting objects. The house is filled with Victorian bric-à-brac, children's paraphernalia and maritime

memorabilia. Despite a lifetime of collecting, the rooms are bright and airy. The light flooding through the windows gives it an unfussy, Scandinavian feeling – appropriate for a North Sea city that was once part of Norway, and whose inhabitants are mostly descended from Viking stock.

TENEMENT HOUSE

OPPOSITE: *Agnes Toward lived at 145 Buccleuch Street from 1911 till 1965. The house has now been restored to what it was like in her day. In the kitchen, the cupboard shown here is still full of jams made by Agnes but never eaten: the oldest is labelled 'Plum 1929'.*

LEFT: *145 Buccleuch Street, one of a row of seven tenements built in 1892. In Scotland the flats in a tenement are known as tenement houses. Agnes Toward's tenement house is on the first floor.*

WHILE THE EIGHTEENTH CENTURY is generally regarded as the zenith of Edinburgh's development, Glasgow's grandest period occurred in the nineteenth. The poet Sir John Betjeman called it 'the greatest Victorian city in the world'. Originally built on the Atlantic trade in tobacco, rum and sugar that flourished in the eighteenth century, the city's prosperity grew with the more profitable businesses of shipbuilding and engineering. By 1901 (the year of Queen Victoria's death) Glasgow and the surrounding districts contained nearly half the population of Scotland – 4.5 million.

The tenement design was originally conceived as a convenient way to house the expanding population in the late 1800s. Buildings mushroomed, especially in the south and south-east of the city, and conditions for the tenants plummeted as landlords, motivated only by profit, squashed more families into less space, neglecting essential repairs on the way. The wealthier, middle classes, however, soon saw the potential of the tenement design and adapted it to suit their more refined requirements. The majority of tenements were constructed in a remarkably short space of time between 1860 and 1910 – and not only in Glasgow. By the end of the nineteenth century, the tenement had become Scotland's most distinctive (and ubiquitous) building type, accommodating within its walls all manner of people and occupations. So while it is true that many tenements became slums, the term in Scotland does not have this connotation, as it does

LEFT: *Another view of the kitchen. The laundry was hung up to dry on the pulley over the range. Ironing was done on the kitchen table using heavy flat irons heated on the range. Hidden from view is a recessed bed, which would have been covered by curtains during the day. The National Trust for Scotland reinstalled the gas lamps, which had been replaced by electricity as recently as 1960.*

RIGHT: *Detail of the bathroom showing the marble-effect washbasin. Few Glaswegians had the luxury of an inside lavatory – most had to share outside privies with their neighbours. The 1892 Act compelling landlords to provide water closets was not always enforced.*

ABOVE: *Small articles of clothing were scrubbed on the zinc-ribbed washboard by the sink and then put through the wringer to squeeze out excess water before being hung up to dry. A variety of cooking implements hang from the shelves, with crockery along the top.*

RIGHT: *The tinted photographs on either side of the fireplace in the parlour show, on the left, Agnes Toward as a child and, on the right, her mother, Mrs Reid. The overmantel was purchased by Agnes from a nearby shop for the sum of £1. 10s (£ 1.50). In many tenement households the parlour was only used for special occasions such as weddings and funerals.*

OPPOSITE: *A set-in bed with its own door in a corner of the parlour. Found only in houses built before 1900, these beds were banned on health grounds. The rosewood piano, a symbol of Victorian gentility, is piled with sheet music of Scottish ballads and other popular songs around the turn of the century. The framed photograph shows Agnes Toward attending a wedding in 1960.*

in England or North America. In working class areas, where the flats had only one or two rooms, they were known as 'single-ends'. At the other end of the scale, much larger flats, with four, five or even more rooms, were built for the affluent. The tenement house (ie, flat) at 145 Buccleuch Street, with its two rooms, kitchen and bathroom, was somewhere in the middle. Dating from the 1890s, the building was red sandstone. This had become extremely fashionable and was used for most of the tenements built at the time, replacing the local white or honey-coloured sandstone of the earlier buildings.

Like most tenements, No. 145 was constructed by speculative builders backed by private investors. Many builders were masons, artisans or tradesmen, and some worked their own quarries. The seven tenements from 71 Garnethill Street to 145 Buccleuch Street cost £13,000 in total. No. 145 was the first to be completed, in December 1892.

Agnes Toward and her mother moved into 145 Buccleuch Street in 1911. After her mother's death in 1939, Agnes stayed on alone – making no major changes, with the exception of the installation of electricity in 1960 – until she was hospitalized in 1965. A habitual hoarder, Agnes found it very hard to throw things away, and for this we must be eternally grateful. She held obsessively onto household bills, rent receipts, recipes, wartime leaflets and newspaper cuttings as well as more personal papers and letters.

The National Trust for Scotland, recognizing its significance for social history, bought the tenement house, replete with most of its Victorian furnishings, in 1982. They reinstalled the gas lighting and, by copying samples of the original decoration carried out by Agnes Toward's mother, were able to redecorate those parts that had been covered over. Today this tenement house offers a uniquely detailed insight into everyday life during the first half of the twentieth century.

THE HILL HOUSE

OPPOSITE: *Looking down into the hall of The Hill House from the stair landing where an open wooden screen plays with light and shadow in the Japanese style. On the walls, narrow strips of stained pine alternate with a stencilled frieze of abstracted 'organic' forms.*

LEFT: *The wrought iron gates leading to the main entrance in the west gable of The Hill House. It was commissioned from Charles Rennie Mackintosh by Walter Blackie. The walls are harled (roughcast with lime and gravel) in light grey and convey a strong impression of the Scottish vernacular tradition.*

A DECADE OR SO AGO, a table designed by Charles Rennie Mackintosh sold for a record $275,000 at Sotheby's, New York. Today people from all over the world visit the house he built for the Glasgow publisher Walter Blackie, overlooking the Firth of Clyde in Helensburgh. Inspired by nature, fired by the ideals of the Arts and Crafts movement and rooted in the vernacular traditions of his native Scotland, Mackintosh's genius was to forge an entirely new style for a new age. Melting the boundaries between design and interior decoration, architecture and art, he applied his vision not only to the design of buildings and furniture, but also to other interior accessories such as cutlery and lamps, tiles, wrought ironwork, fireplaces and mantelpieces. Although now acknowledged by the Scots as their greatest and most innovative architect and designer, during his lifetime he was reviled or simply ignored by most of his countrymen, while receiving ever greater recognition abroad.

Mackintosh's early career boded well. He was a brilliant student at the Glasgow School of Art, and with the commission to redesign the art school in 1896, his professional life seemed assured. But after a decade of great creativity, fewer and fewer commissions came his way and, deeply resentful at the lack of recognition in his native city, Mackintosh finally left Glasgow in 1913, never to return. After a period in London he abandoned architecture for good, retreating to the South of France where he lived until his death at the age of 60 in 1928.

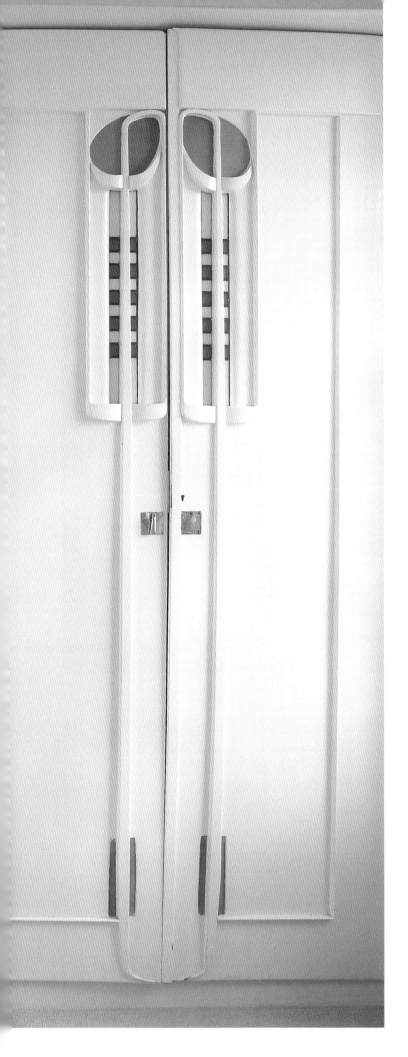

LEFT: *One of a pair of ebonized oak ladderback chairs stands out dramatically against the all-white paintwork of the L-shaped main bedroom, designed for Mrs Blackie. The touches of pink on the carved cupboard doors soften the otherwise stark effect.*

BELOW: *Another part of the bedroom, showing the elegant cheval mirror. As in the drawing room, the pink squares on the translucent curtains echo other details in either colour or form.*

LEFT: *A lamp in the drawing room. The pink and green organic design of the lampshade is echoed in the wall stencils and curtains, while the lamp column incorporates still more squares. A perfectionist, Mackintosh sought total control, designing tables and chairs, clocks, lamps, keys and cutlery. He would make as many sketches for a single spoon as for a dining room table.*

RIGHT: *Over the small
jewellery cabinet, with a
different lock and key for
each drawer, a shuttered
window opens into a
curved alcove. On sunny
days the tiny squares of
pink glass fill this part of
the room with a rosy glow.
The stencilled roses
entwined with trellising on
the walls was only revealed
in 1989 when the National
Trust for Scotland removed
layers of white paint.*

ABOVE: *A 1905 clock,
originally intended for the
drawing room, now sits on
the mantelpiece in the
library. Made of ebony and
stained sycamore with
ivory inlay, it has painted
Roman numerals and is
supported on 16 sycamore
columns set into a square
base. Its design was
modified and repeated
several times by
Mackintosh.*

The role played by his few patrons was crucial to his limited output. Walter Blackie, already familiar with the evolving Glasgow style, commissioned Mackintosh to build The Hill House after he had bought a plot of land in Helensburgh in 1902. The two men liked and respected one another and shared many ideas. Rejecting pastiche, they both preferred 'a plain style' that was sensitive to the vernacular precedent set by earlier Scottish buildings, 'the architecture of our own country, just as much Scotch as we are ourselves', as Mackintosh expressed it. The rather stark exterior of The Hill House is consistent with this, but the exterior was secondary to the interior plans. Before starting work, Mackintosh spent some time with the Blackie family, observing their way of life and their requirements so that he could build their house around them, from the inside out. It was only after the interior plans had been agreed upon that he designed the elevations.

Blackie was very impressed with the care that Mackintosh took over every detail of his house. 'To the larder, kitchen, laundry, etc, he gave minute attention to fit them for practical needs, and always pleasingly designed. Every detail, inside as well as outside, received his careful, I might say, loving attention.' Blackie found himself falling 'more and more in love' with details at first discarded for reasons of economy, and then reprieved.

Mackintosh's designs reflect his abiding interest in symbolism through nature. Many are rich in organic motifs: roses and cabbages, stems and bulbs. As a child, he wandered

around the countryside sketching wildflowers, plants and trees, as well as buildings. In this way architecture and nature became fused together quite naturally. A further influence on The Hill House, as on his other work, was that of Japan. On the small stairway landing, Mackintosh used an open screen in the Japanese fashion to create bands of light and shadow, like sunlight falling through trees.

Like all creative lateral thinkers, Mackintosh was fond of transmuting forms from one medium to others. His sketchbooks are filled with designs later adapted to other contexts: for example, the massive and asymmetrically angled chimney by the main entrance on the west front recalls his study of Kent oasthouses, with their unevenly angled tops. His frequent use of a pierced-through square pattern, such as those on the front door, are reminiscent of an open square-chequered barn window at Saxlingham, Norfolk.

Mackintosh regarded architecture as the 'the mother of the arts' and sought a holistic vision that would integrate and unify all the arts under its mantle in a dynamic yet harmonic whole. As early as 1904, the Berlin designer Hermann Muthesius had written of the 'almost mystical sense of peace' in Mackintosh's rooms. 'Colour used in this frugal way has, so to speak, its status raised… the effect is as of a jewel.' It is disquieting to think that had the mirror of appreciation been raised in his own time in his native Scotland, many more jewels might be shining today.

ABOVE: *On the left of the entrance to the main bedroom is a sitting room area. The fireplace with its steel surround contains three pink enamelled tiles whose design echoes the carvings on the bedroom's white wardrobes. The linear design on the built-in leather-back seat reflects that of the curtains – only the other way up.*

5. INVENTIVE

TRADITIONS

INVENTIVE
TRADITIONS

KINLOCHMOIDART

OPPOSITE: *A view towards the south-facing end of the hall, which is now the billiard room. Stag heads preside over Chinese brass ensigns and a Siamese chair – trophies that symbolize both Robert Stewart's lairdly aspirations and his Far Eastern connections. The heavily embossed green wallpaper and all the panelling are original. The portrait is of Nino Stewart's grandmother.*

LEFT: *Designed and built in 1883–4 by William Leiper for Robert Stewart, Kinlochmoidart is an accomplished essay in the Scots Baronial style. This picture shows the west side of the house with the Moidart hills beyond. Proud of his supposed royal ancestry, Robert Stewart insisted on a castle that would evoke the romance of the Jacobites, while relating to its dramatic Highland setting.*

WHEN THE PRESENT OWNER, NINO STEWART, inherited Kinlochmoidart in 1972, experts advised her to demolish it without further ado. The place was draughty and damp, and dry rot had penetrated the rafters. One phone call, and the bulldozers would be on their way, but Nino Stewart resisted. She recognized vandalism for what it was, even when urged by lawyers, accountants and architects. Thanks to her vision and tenacity – and the generous grants she was later able to obtain from Historic Scotland – the house has been saved and its future at the heart of one of the most beautiful Highland estates secured.

Kinlochmoidart, at the head of Loch Moidart in the western Highlands, lies in one of the least accessible parts of Scotland's west coast. Formerly known as *Garbh-criochan* ('the rough bounds'), the estate, with its wooded hills and open parkland, belonged for nearly three centuries to a sept (subdivision) of the Clan MacDonald, hereditary Lords of the Isles. In the rising of 1745, Donald MacDonald of Kinlochmoidart sided with Bonnie Prince Charlie. After raising his father's standard at nearby Glenfinnan, the Young Pretender stayed at Kinlochmoidart for a week. In the end, the rebellion failed, and as a punishment – and a warning to other would-be rebels – the estate was forfeited and the castle burned to the ground in the 'Great Wasting' of 1746. Though the MacDonalds rebuilt their home in the late eighteenth century, their fortunes never recovered, and the estate was put on the market in 1882.

ABOVE: *A Madonna and
Child in the style of
Murillo, commissioned for
the house, dominates the
main staircase lit by the
huge leaded-light window.
The embossed wallpaper
used in the hall continues
up the stairs. Above the
picture rail a pattern of
gilded stencilling stands
out dramatically against
a russet background.*

OPPOSITE: *The dark tones
of the panelled main hall
are lightened by a gilt
mirror and two round
brass plaques above a
Renaissance-style granite
fireplace. The staircase is
divided from the hall by an
arched screen supported
by elaborately carved
wooden columns.*

ABOVE: *Detail of the stencilled
frieze of stylized peacocks and
thistles on the upstairs landing.
The gilded patterns gleam as they
catch the light, a* tour de force
*that reflects Leiper's art school
training in Paris.*

RIGHT: *The lobby at the top of the short staircase is lit from the right by an intricately glazed leaded oriel window. The walls, like those in the hall into which it leads, are panelled in dark polished wood with embossed green wallpaper above the dado rail. Flanking the oak chest-of-drawers are two Japanese ensigns.*

BELOW: *Detail of the dining room fireplace which is built into a half-barrel-vaulted inglenook. On the mantelpiece stands a nineteenth-century French ormolu clock and a pair of matching candelabra.*

It was bought by Robert Stewart, a wealthy Glaswegian distiller who was also the first person to import frozen meat into Britain from New Zealand and Australia. Inspired by its romantic setting and Jacobite associations and fancying a connection – however tenuous – with Scotland's doomed royal house (which was spelt Stewart prior to 1603), he bought the demesne with its 6,000 hectares (15,000 acres) of shooting and anchorage for his yachts. Desiring a house appropriate to his wealth and magnificent new surroundings, Stewart abandoned the existing dwelling and commissioned the Glasgow architect William Leiper to design something entirely new and grand.

Working mainly in the west of Scotland, Leiper was a sensitive exponent of the Scottish Baronial style (which he preferred to call 'Old Scots'). But he also favoured other idioms, as can be seen in several villas he designed in and around Helensburgh, where he lived. The design of one such villa, Dalmore, in the tower-house tradition, became the inspiration for Kinlochmoidart. Robert Stewart perhaps visited Dalmore and was so impressed that he requested an exact copy, on a grander scale, for his country seat.

Standing proudly in its Highland setting, Kinlochmoidart blends with the surrounding landscape through carefully chosen materials – locally quarried grey whinstone complemented by imported red sandstone dressing. The impregnable tower-house form is accentuated by a scarcity of windows.

Most of the original 1880s furnishings and decoration have survived, and the level of craftsmanship is superb. Apart from the bedrooms, which are plastered and wallpapered, the interior is characterized by a dark richness created by the generous use of polished wood panelling, timber screens and heavily embossed wallpapers. Carpets, brass plaques and inlaid oak furniture add dashes of light and colour and a sense of discreet opulence.

In his interior design Leiper recognized the building's double function as shooting lodge and country house, providing clearly delineated spaces for the multifarious pursuits of a rich Victorian family. His hierarchical arrangement of space and function greatly simplified the task of restoration. In the late 1980s, the architect Kit Martin, a specialist in country-house conversions, produced a sensitive scheme of subdivision, enabling the house to earn its keep with apartments for holiday letting while remaining Nino Stewart's home. The firm of Simpson and Brown took on the decade-long job of restoring the fabric of the house. Once again Kinlochmoidart can welcome its guests in style.

ABOVE: *One of the guest bedrooms with, at the end, a tiled curtained alcove containing a large, luxurious bath. To its left is a built-in cupboard cum chest-of-drawers designed by William Leiper, who redesigned Kinlochmoidart in the 1880s. Middle Eastern ceramic vases stand on a table at the end of the canopied Victorian brass bed.*

INVENTIVE
TRADITIONS

ARDPATRICK

OPPOSITE: *View from the dining room, through the hall to the 'first dwych' (drawing room). The embroidered squares on the wall are marriage mats from Zaire. The oil painting above the settee is of Caroline Kenneil, by her mother-in-law, Esther ('Pete') Kenneil. The Regency-style arches are part of the refurbishments undertaken in the 1920s.*

LEFT: *The house from the garden side. Much of the original wall, dating from 1769, has been hidden by a late nineteenth-century balcony with steps leading to the walled garden. The tower with its conical tiled roof contains a spiral staircase connecting the central block with the nineteenth-century wing.*

THE BEST WAY TO ARRIVE AT ARDPATRICK is by boat across West Loch Tarbert, a rough and sometimes treacherous stretch of water separating the Kintyre peninsula from Knapdale. Set on a rocky promontory amid ancient woodlands and fields on the south-western corner of Knapdale, in Argyll, with inspiring views of the Paps of Jura, the Mull of Kintyre and sometimes the Antrim coast of Northern Ireland (on a clear day), the demesne is virtually an island – a relic of an older Argyll, infused with a Gaelic magic that has disappeared elsewhere. Though it is thought that Patrick may be a corruption of Federich – a local name – the Irish resonances are appropriate. Maps from the days when the Clan MacDonald held sway on both sides of the Irish Sea show Antrim as part of Scotland. Centuries before that, the ancient kingdom of Strathclyde was one of three places on the British mainland (the others being Wales and Somerset) from where it is thought that Ireland's patron saint might have hailed.

The estate has more than 12 hectares (30 acres) of primary oak forest, which once grew all over the western Highlands. Honed by Atlantic gales, the gnarled little trees mould themselves to the contours of the land, creating a delicate canopy whose colours change with the seasons along with the bracken and heather. Sadly, the natural seasoning to which the oak was subjected made it an ideal source for charcoal used in the smelting process before the coal-based Industrial Revolution got under way. The demand for cannonballs and cannon, fuelled by England's wars with Scotland's old ally France, led

to the almost complete disappearance of the indigenous oaks. Protected by the rough waters of the Jura Sound and the absence of a decent road, the oak woods of Ardpatrick are almost unique.

Esther ('Pete') and Walter Kenneil acquired Ardpatrick in 1946. Pete Wolton (née Nelson, of the Edinburgh publishing house Thomas Nelson) was already married, with two children, when she met Walter Kahn, an American banker, on a trip to New York during the Second World War. Having no cash because of wartime restrictions, she had brought with her just one valuable possession, a Stradivarius violin. A crooked dealer – who surreptitiously shifted the instrument's bridge to flaw its tone – offered her a derisory sum. Walter, a friend of a friend, spotted the deception and got her a decent price. The couple forged their alliance in an unusual manner, by changing both their surnames to the Scottish name Kenneil. At Ardpatrick they were able to live an idyllic life which set them apart from the rather more strait-laced gentry to be found in Argyll at that time. The estate now belongs to Walter and Pete's three children and their families.

Set among majestic beeches and elms, Ardpatrick has gone through many transformations. The original house, which was probably built in the seventeenth century and may have been what is now the south-facing façade of the north wing, was one of many belonging to the Dukes of Argyll. Between 1769 and 1776, the Duke's factor (steward), Angus MacAlister, greatly enlarged it, adding the building that now forms the central block, as well as a second wing on the south side. MacAlister appears to have overreached

RIGHT: *A lantern from an Indian temple hangs over the dining room table. The carpet hanging on the wall behind the Regency sideboard was brought from Kundiz, Afghanistan. To the left of the late nineteenth-century mirror (partly concealed) hangs a Matisse lithograph. The painting to the right of the mirror is a landscape by Jock MacDonald.*

BELOW: *The drawing room showing part of a Russian bed adapted to make a canopied upholstered bench. The dove with an olive branch, embroidered with beads, was found in a local junk shop. The quilt hanging behind the piano is early nineteenth-century American. The wood and gesso wicker-backed chair came from Sweden.*

151

ABOVE: *The hall, with the dining room beyond, viewed through a Regency-style arch which was part of the 1920s interior refurbishment. The wood and cane settee is nineteenth-century French, as is the painted wardrobe in the dining room.*

OPPOSITE: *Walking sticks stand in a milk churn in the passage leading to the former service wing, created when the dining room was enlarged.*

himself, and the estate was bought from his creditors in 1798 by Walter Campbell of Shawfield and Islay. It remained with this branch of the Campbells for more than a century, during which time further enlargements were made. In the 1920s a new owner, John Birkmyre, a Greenock rope-maker, made additional alterations, installing triple picture windows on the ground floor.

Like the façade, the interior has gone through many changes during the past two centuries. Its pleasantly Bohemian atmosphere – more Irish than Scottish – was imparted by Pete Kenneil, a talented artist, who allowed her children to run around barefoot before sending them south to be 'civilized' at English public schools. The bohemian tradition has been kept up by her son Alastair and his wife, Caroline, also a painter, who have filled the house with hangings and artefacts from their travels in Asia and Africa and furniture from Caroline's family home in Shropshire. The patina of its interior design, from its original Georgian austerities through 1920s neoclassicism hung with ethnic mementos, imparts to Ardpatrick an unusually eclectic flavour in a land where the lairdly imagination rarely extends beyond sporting prints, trophies and chintz.

INVENTIVE
TRADITIONS

ST MARY'S FARM

ABOVE: *View of the farmhouse from the south. The outbuildings on the right have eighteenth-century russet pantiles from Holland, brought up the Forth by Dutch ships.*

OPPOSITE: *The yellow kitchen. On the ledge over the Aga, which replaced the original range, is a selection of Scottish tin cups and jugs, each inscribed with a brass plaque. One says 'Oor Wee Pet 1886', another 'Annies Wee Bath', and a third 'Dinae Scald The Cream'.*

S T MARY'S FARM NESTLES among giant rolling cornfields in Fife. Built low and following the lie of the land, the little farmhouse in its dip is almost invisible until you turn into the track leading down to it. Surrounded by a cluster of russet-tiled and rough stone outbuildings, everything appears at ease with the landscape. It is hard to believe that anything has changed for generations. Dating from 1810, the south-facing dressed stone façade is of the simplest design, with a central door, a window either side and a chimney at each end. The only decorative concessions are the rusticated angle quoins and two plain columns supporting a lintel over the entrance.

When Carolyn Scott and Michael Innes bought their house in 1987 it was derelict. But the farmhouse suited them. Carolyn, an antiques dealer and interior designer, needed outbuildings in which she could store her larger items of furniture. Michael, a garden

155

ABOVE: *Nineteenth-century Scottish chessboards with tartan decoration hang on the walls of the upstairs landing. Popular in Victorian times, they were made to many different shapes and designs.*

RIGHT: *Looking down the hall from the entrance, with the kitchen at the far end. An old tartan shepherd's shawl and a vase of geraniums complement the delicate lime-green walls, mixed by an artist friend. On the left is an unusual antique oak cupboard. The banister rail is the only piece of original woodwork left in the house.*

LEFT: *The carved wooden panels, stripped of layers of varnish and paint, give the bathroom an original feel. Above the frieze is a selection of pressed ferns from Australia and New Zealand, part of a Victorian collection. The traditional Orkney chair, made of driftwood and sea grass, is designed to keep out draughts.*

BELOW: *A large Victorian brass bed dominates the guest bedroom. It is covered with an antique red and white patchwork quilt. The built-in cupboard doors are old window shutters.*

designer, required office space and could, with time, create his own garden on the land around the house. The farm is within easy reach of Edinburgh, where both Carolyn and Michael conduct some of their business.

The house was in such a poor state that it would have been easier to knock it down and rebuild from scratch. Although they were determined to preserve as much of the original fabric as possible, it transpired that virtually nothing could be salvaged. After decades of neglect, the rot had penetrated everywhere. The roof and the top of the walls had to be ripped down and rebuilt, and inside was just as bad. In the end the only piece of original wood left was the banister rail. Everything else had to be sought out and salvaged from reclamation yards. Even the hall flagstones were beyond repair (or had vanished). Replacements were eventually found in an old stable block that was being demolished. Altogether it took them more than a year, living in rented accommodation nearby, to make the house habitable.

The temporary discomforts, however, have been amply rewarded. Inside, the charm of the house is its lack of pretentiousness. The room colours – yellow and blue in the kitchen, a subtle lime green in the hall and on the landing – suggest a lightness of spirit. The effect is enhanced by flowers, most of which are grown in the small conservatory adjoining the kitchen. The combination of flowers (especially geraniums), old textiles and an eclectic mix of antique furniture gives the house a special flavour strengthened by the patina of time. Nothing has changed since Carolyn and Michael finally moved in, nearly a decade ago. As Carolyn sees it, 'The first inclination is invariably the best.'

INVENTIVE
TRADITIONS

KILLEAN

OPPOSITE: *Two eighteenth-century portraits hang either side of an early nineteenth-century Rococo bracket clock over the original dining-room mantelpiece. The miniatures beneath show the sitters in later life. Flanking the fireplace is a pair of late seventeenth-century Italian-style walnut armchairs with carved acanthus finials. The green scumbled and glazed walls were done by interior designer Amy Rosco, daughter of the owner.*

LEFT: *View of Killean House showing the Isle of Gigha across the Sound. In the distance can be seen the Paps of Jura. Completed in the early 1880s, Killean reflects the divergent tastes of the architects Sir John Burnet, exemplifying the Scots Baronial tradition, and his son and pupil, John James, who was closely associated with the Scottish Arts and Crafts movement.*

KINTYRE, THE LEGGY PENINSULA IN ARGYLL, extends down the west coast of central Scotland and culminates in a spectacular headland overlooking the Mull, from where Ireland is clearly visible. It consists largely of rugged moorland with long, lonely beaches interspersed with cliffs and strange rock formations. Here, one is truly 'out on a limb'. Remoter (by road) than many more obviously 'picturesque' parts of northern Argyll, it is often said of Kintyre that it has 'a Lowland population in a Highland setting'. Responsibility lies with the Earl of Argyll, who initiated a controversial 'plantation' of settlers from the Ayrshire Lowlands after 1650. Over one hundred years of bitter feuding between the MacDonald and Campbell clans, coupled with the ravages of a terrible plague in 1647, had decimated the population.

Around 1875, James Macalister Hall, who had made his fortune in India as a merchant and shipowner, decided to build himself a dream house on Kintyre. Like other wealthy Glaswegians, he was attracted by the peninsula's location. Although Kintyre's west coast, with its Hebridean seas and islands, is notoriously treacherous, its east coast together with the Island of Arran can be seen as a distant outlier of the Firth of Clyde – and even of Glasgow. The boats moored on the east coast at Tarbert, the narrowest point of Kintyre, combined with the sheltered inland waters, made it comparatively easy to escape the smog-infested city and enjoy long summer evenings with beautiful ocean views and pure Atlantic air.

INVENTIVE TRADITIONS

KILLEAN

RIGHT: *This view of the circular library on the ground floor of the tower was taken from the smaller tower adjoining it. A late Regency drum-top table supported on a triform column and plinth echoes the circular shape. The blue wallpaper and matching paintwork are original, as are most of the books and soft furnishings.*

KILLEAN

RIGHT: *Looking through to the drawing room from the hall. The portrait is of Mrs McKenzie, sister of James Macalister Hall, who built Killean. It was painted in 1894 by William Charles Wontner. To the right of the table stands a gilt-bronze Art Nouveau serpentine lamp after Edgar Brandt.*

BELOW: *The William Morris wallpaper sets the tone for the drawing room. A sixteenth-century painting of 'St George and the Dragon' by a follower of Martin de Vos hangs on the wall.*

Hall bought two adjoining estates opposite the Island of Gigha on the west coast, first Tangy and soon after, in 1873, Killean. At Killean, he was content initially to enlarge the existing house to designs by the Scottish architect John Burnet, but as soon as it was finished, in 1875, everything was burnt down except the porch. Hall lost no time: a 'magnificent new mansion house' was conceived on a different site, the plans for which were exhibited at the Royal Scottish Academy in 1876. The new house, probably finished in the early 1880s, is an

intriguing architectural dialogue between John Burnet, who worked in a mid-Victorian Scottish Baronial style, and his better-known son and pupil, John James Burnet. The latter became a leading Scottish exponent of the Arts and Crafts movement. John James completed his architectural training at the École des Beaux Arts in Paris, and most probably helped his father at Killean on his return in 1877.

LEFT: *Detail of the dining room. The green glazed wall sets off to advantage an early eighteenth-century portrait of a lady holding a sheet of music by a harpsichord.*

BELOW: *View of the Arran bedroom. All the bedrooms at Killean are named after neighbouring islands, some of which can be seen from the windows. Behind the Victorian bed stands a George IV mahogony gentleman's wardrobe. The carpet is Persian.*

The harsh, asymmetrical outline, with its see-through tower and corbelled projection, is steeped in the mannerisms of the 1860s and 1870s, and is probably the work of the father. It is typically mid-Victorian, as is the generally vertical massing of the living end of the house and the long, low servants' wing adjoining it. However, the spacing of the windows, the two-storey pavilion containing the main entrance, with its high French mansard roof, as well as the surprisingly well-lit hall, suggest the work of John James. In fact, very little of the simple but sophisticated exterior detailing has the hallmark of the father, and some of the interior details are quite idiosyncratic, giving the impression of a young architect trying his hand for the very first time. But though the division of work between father and son at the main house is far from clear, some of the estate cottages have a remarkably orthodox Arts and Crafts flavour,

The present owner, Keith Schellenberg, who bought the house and estate in 1995, was inspired, like James Macalister Hall, by the remoteness of its location. He also likes yachts. Renovating the cottages first (which provide an income as holiday lets) he then focused on Killean House which, apart from some major bathroom restorations, was mostly a matter of refurbishment. The house and estate cottages received a Commended Award from the Association for the Protection of Rural Scotland in 1998.

INVENTIVE TRADITIONS

MELSETTER HOUSE

ABOVE: *Set in rolling farmland on the island of Hoy, Melsetter House is sited on a promontory between Scapa Flow and the Pentland Firth. The only trees on the island, and the hill behind the house, provide some shelter from the savage North Sea gales.*

OPPOSITE: *The hall, with Buddhist gongs in the foreground, showing the upper landing and steps leading down to the main entrance on a lower level.*

HOY IS THE MOST SPECTACULAR OF THE ORKNEY ISLANDS. With its rugged moorland and towering sandstone cliffs overlooking the Pentland Firth (one of the roughest and most dangerous sea-passages in the world) it is the least populated of the larger islands – a fact that still makes it attractive to settlers with romantic inclinations. In 1898 a wealthy Englishman, Thomas Middlemore, sold his factories and bought the Melsetter estate, comprising Hoy and three smaller islands. He and his Scottish wife, Theodosia, were keen supporters of the Arts and Crafts movement, founded by William Morris in the 1880s. The Middlemores invited a leading exponent of the movement, the architect and designer William Lethaby, to adapt and extend the existing eighteenth-century steading (farmstead) at Melsetter. The result is a glorious surprise: an architectural gem that sparkles with silvery light, or, as William Morris's daughter May described it, 'a sort of fairy palace on the edge of the great northern seas'.

Like Morris and other pioneering socialists, Lethaby believed in the redemptive power of labour and the wisdom embodied in craftsmanship. Eleven masons were brought over from Kirkwall, the Orkney capital, to work on the locally quarried sandstone and to dress

INVENTIVE
TRADITIONS

MELSETTER HOUSE

RIGHT: *The drawing room, with its simple white panelling and windows positioned to capture the changing light throughout the day, has a distinctly Georgian feel. In contrast to the exponents of Victorian Gothic, the architect William Lethaby, who remodelled the house, approved of unfussy classicism.*

OPPOSITE: *The passage leading to the hall. On the left is the original serving room now used as the kitchen. Lethaby raised the ceiling of the original basement kitchen to allow staff a view of the garden. Visitors commented on the classless atmosphere encouraged by the original owners, the Middlemores, with everyone joining in fruit picking and jam making.*

BELOW: *The drawing room fireplace with its original tiles of birds and flowers. The marble surround has been split and joined to emphasize the organic quality of its original liquid state. The panelling above is a seascape by the Orcadian artist Sylvia Wishart.*

the mullions, chimneys and gables that offset the traditional harled walls – like the trimming on an Edwardian suit. Unlike so many Victorian mansions that set out to dominate the skyline, the design is carefully understated.

A similar blend of tradition grafted to the aesthetics of contemporary taste informs the interior, which has a luminous modern feel. Large ceremonial fireplaces are offset by oak floors and soft white floor-to-ceiling panelling. Rooms are carefully oriented to maximize the potentialities of the silvery northern light. Windows are judiciously placed to capture the sun. As the late Jo Grimond, Orkney's most famous politician, put it, the interior atmosphere 'seems very friendly, not only to its occupants, but to the very air. The light falls in shafts; spaces in passages, on the stairs and in the rooms seem to have shape.'

The Middlemores died without children. During the Second World War, the house, which is conveniently situated near the great natural harbour of Scapa Flow, home of the North Sea Fleet, was requisitioned by the Royal Navy. After the war the house and home farm were bought by the Setters, former tenants of the estate. It now belongs to their children: Hugh farms the land and Elsie, a district nurse, looks after the house. Helped by grants from Historic Scotland, they have kept most of the original fabrics and furnishings intact. Concerts are sometimes held in the drawing room. The outbuildings have been converted into charming holiday flats, and architectural students are sometimes invited to stay in the house. The atmosphere is contagious. Aloof from the vagaries of fashion, the Middlemore legacy lives on. Lethaby's 'fairy palace' could not have wished for a better fate.

THE OLD MANOR

OPPOSITE: *The murals on the top floor of the Old Manor date from 1748, when the house was constructed. Thought to be the work of the firm of Norries of Haddington who specialized in interior wall decoration, they are unusually executed with oils on plaster. The doll's house comes from T'bilisi, Georgia – though the style is Scandinavian.*

LEFT: *The Old Manor from the garden. Built for Archibald Shiells, a fruit merchant, it was extended in the nineteenth century with a service wing and outbuildings. The More Gordons had these knocked down in 1974, restoring the house to its original proportions.*

THE OLD MANOR STANDS IN AN ACRE OF WOODLAND GARDEN overlooking a river with fine views of woods and hills beyond. When it was first built in the mid-eighteenth century it must have seemed like an upstart compared with the aristocratic country mansions designed by the likes of William Adam and his sons. Its plain rubble walls, stone angle quoins and slightly disproportionate height, while not necessarily at odds with the classical façade, reveal its less than refined origins. Despite its imposing appearance it is a burgher's house – a status symbol built with 'new money'.

The eighteenth century was a golden age for the middle classes in Scotland, despite the political upheavals of 1715 and 1745 – but the Highlanders lost out. The clan system that had sustained them for centuries was destroyed, in many cases by their own chiefs who benefited from collaboration with English power. The burghers, however, profited from the Union and the Hanoverian peace that followed the demise of the Stuarts. While dispossessed Highlanders settled in America or enlisted (willingly or otherwise) in Britain's imperial armies – becoming a crucial element in the expanding empire – a newly confident middle class took advantage of the commercial opportunities brought by peace. In the age of Adam Smith and David Hume, the middle class came to dominate both trade and industry, and the realm of ideas. The Old Manor, built in the mid-eighteenth century by Archibald Shiells, a merchant who made his money in the fruit trade, is an embodiment of this success.

ABOVE: *One of the bathrooms on the first floor, created from a dressing room at the front of the house. Its windows flanking the painted wooden mantelpiece make it exceptionally light. The old fireplace has been covered with a Japanese lacquer panel.*

RIGHT: *On the mantelpiece in the green bedroom, a Victorian Staffordshire figurine – one of a pair given by Harry More Gordon to his wife as a wedding present – reclines next to a tree made in China from semi-precious stones.*

OPPOSITE: *Two jugs, from the collection used by Harry More Gordon as props in his paintings, stand in a bathroom, one reflected in an Edwardian shaving mirror. The apple-shaped cabinet standing on the French mahogany escritoire was exchanged for one of Harry's paintings. The landscape is by W Gillies.*

ABOVE: *The drawing room is full of light, increased by the absence of curtains. The windows were extended in the nineteenth century and the shutters have been glazed on the inside to reflect lights at night. The alcove, with its collection of mostly eighteenth-century porcelain, was originally a claret cupboard. The settee is Regency.*

RIGHT: *Detail of the drawing room with fitted bookshelves and Art Nouveau bookbindings. The vase is Scottish, made from Monart glass. The hand-printed wallpaper is by Coles of London.*

Today, a century and a half later, the home of this erstwhile parvenu seems charmingly unpretentious: a comfortable, but not unduly grand, family house which has adapted itself to the times without fuss, becoming gracefully attuned to the rhythms of modern living.

The top floor of the house is decorated with unsophisticated wall paintings that complement the plain, rather rustic exterior. Depicting hunting life (fishing, shooting and stalking), these wall decorations were designed, one suspects, to enhance the client's social status. The genre was particularly popular with middle-class Lowlanders who were keen to associate themselves with the gentry, and many an eighteenth-century house was adorned with them. As well as being decorative, they were a good deal cheaper to install than wooden panelling. One family firm, Norries of Haddington, kept up the tradition of wall painting for several generations. The vast majority of these paintings have now been lost, painted over or covered with wallpaper – the Old Manor's collection is the largest to have survived.

LEFT: *The new ground-floor kitchen, created by removing the partitions of three smaller rooms, replaced the old kitchen in the basement. It is now the family's principal living room. The Victorian kitchen table was bought for ten shillings (50p) at a local sale. The Arts and Crafts chair by Ernest Gimson was rescued from a junk yard. The porcelain female bust on the mantelpiece is Sèvres, c. 1870, one of a pair symbolizing Alsace and Lorraine.*

Harry and Marianne More Gordon stumbled across the Old Manor almost by accident. Having lived and worked in London as a graphic designer, Harry had one week to go before beginning a new job teaching illustration. The elderly general and his wife who owned the house obviously liked them, and the deal was clinched overnight. According to Marianne the couple had very little money – certainly not enough to furnish a whole Palladian house complete with ugly Victorian extensions. However, this was the 1960s and no one was buying old furniture. They bought the beds, bedding and much of the rest of the furniture, including the scrubbed kitchen table, for £100 when the contents of a nearby house went up for auction. The beds arrived in pieces and took weeks to put together, but they were all of good-quality brass. The rest of the furniture came from local junk shops. These were the days when Victorian wardrobes, quilts, paisleys and anything Art Deco – in fact, almost anything 'old' – could be picked up for virtually nothing. Marianne once discovered a hand-woven linen sheet with an 1815 laundry mark being used as a decorator's dust sheet.

Bravely taking on the planners, the More Gordons knocked down the Victorian extensions – a service wing and some coal sheds. Apart from adapting two small rooms into bathrooms, it was a case of piecemeal renovation. The ridge on which the house is situated exposes it to icy gales. Harry and Marianne's daughter, Domenica, recall that when they first moved in, it wasn't unusual to wake up with frost on the inside of the windowpanes and the glass of water by the bed frozen. Efforts at insulation with copper

RIGHT: *Detail of Harry More Gordon's studio, originally a sitting room, showing his portrait of Domenica, aged 18. In an unintended decorative conceit she is posed against the fireplace in the same room, with another of Harry's paintings above. Many of the objects on the chest have featured as props in Harry's portraits.*

OPPOSITE: *The downstairs passage leading from the hall, with Harry More Gordon's studio on the left. The painting is by the Scottish artist John Mooney. A vase of tulips and a jug stand deceptively on the table – closer inspection reveals them to be soft sculptures by Marianne More Gordon.*

draught-excluders resulted in a 'cacophony of hoots, whines and operatic screams'. In the worst-affected room, the drawing room, conversation became impossible when the wind was strong. The only certain way of keeping out draughts was to glue the windows shut.

Thirty years later the house is snugger and more comfortable, but magpie habits originally born of necessity persist. The Old Manor is full of interesting bric-a-brac that reflects its owners' eclectic tastes and infallible eyes. Marianne, who originally trained as a sculptor, now works exclusively in textiles. She makes textile portraits and slightly surreal soft sculptures of solid or familiar objects such as jugs and flowers.

Many of the objects in the house – including a large collection of interesting jugs – feature as props in Harry More Gordon's still lifes and portraits. Specializing in watercolours, Harry is now one of Scotland's best-known portraitists. Preferring to paint his subjects in their own surroundings, he believes that one can tell a great deal about people from their possessions. Judging from the choice of objects with which the More Gordons have surrounded themselves, theirs is a gently exuberant household, inventive and visually aware – a shaft of sunlight under brooding Scottish skies.

LEFT: *A renovated fisherman's cottage in Cromarty in the north-east Highlands.*

INDEX

Figures in italics refer to illustrations or captions